What the Bible says about Marriage, Divorce, and Remarriage.

by

Robert

Breaker

III

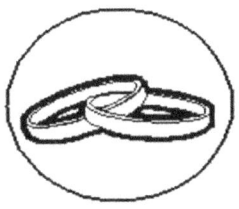

Copyright © 2001 by Robert Breaker

Reprinted 2011.

*What the Bible Says About Marriage,
Divorce, and Remarriage*
by Robert Breaker

Printed in the United States of America

ISBN 9781619040441

All rights reserved solely by the author. The author guarantees all contents are original and do not infringe upon the legal rights of any other person or work. No part of this book may be reproduced in any form without the permission of the author. The views expressed in this book are not necessarily those of the publisher.

Unless otherwise indicated, Bible quotations are taken from the King James version.

www.xulonpress.com

Breaker's Publications

What the Bible Says About Marriage, Divorce and Remarriage

By Robert Breaker

3rd Edition

Preface

Dear reader, the title of this book is, "*What THE BIBLE SAYS About Marriage, Divorce, and Remarriage*." The author's intent was to put forth a booklet about this afore mentioned topic from a Bible standpoint, and use only the Authorized King James Bible as his basis. No opinions or teachings of man will be presented within this work as higher than the authority of the words of the living God. What God says has and always will be higher than man's thoughts or ideas about the subject, as he is the one who instituted marriage, and his words should be heeded when we look at the topic.

This booklet is written in an attempt (and a feeble one at that) to show the reader what God says and thinks about Marriage, Divorce, and Remarriage.

The writer of this booklet does not claim to be God, nor know all that God knows (not even close). But, he does want to learn all that God has for him. And, the only way to do so, is to read and believe God's holy words. And, where the Bible says one thing, and man's opinions, traditions, or ideas say another, the author of this book would rather believe and practice what God says!

Psalm 118:8 says, "*It is* **better to trust in the LORD than to put confidence in man.**" And, my desire for this booklet is that those reading it will trust God and his words about the subject over those of man (myself included).

This book is written for several reasons. First and foremost, being that far too many books on the subject do not go indepth or in detail enough about the *spiritual aspect* of marriage, and its *wonderful type* of Christ and the Church. Some will approach the subject, and use the Bible, but they fail to even attempt to go deep enough to show the man's duties as a type of Christ, and the woman's duties as a type of the Church. I hope to do just that, and open one's eyes to the spiritual type that Marriage is in the Bible, and what it was instituted to be.

My desire is that this will help married couples in their Marriage relationship, as they see who they are a type of, and how they are supposed to treat one another.

Second, this work was done because of the vast ignorance and misconception by the majority of Christians (as well as the lost world) about marriage, and how a marriage should work according to God. Far too many have forgotten that Marriage was ordained by God himself, and was instituted not only for mankind to be "*fruitful and multiply and replenish the earth*" (Genesis 1:28), but also to keep society moral, and for homes to stay together for the sake of the children. Not only that, but marriage was set up for each spouse to love and comfort the other, and by so doing, they will fulfill the needs of their partner, and find fulfillment themselves.

Far too many people today don't know how to have a marriage, much less a godly Christian home. I hope that the verses of Scripture quoted in this booklet will be enlightening to the reader. And, I hope that the reader will heed the commands of God presented herein so that they might have a wonderful marriage and honor God as they enjoy their spouse's company.

Finally, this booklet was written because the author has seen far too many divorces among Christians. Too many people today don't look at marriage as something that is for life. They approach it with the attitude of, *"if it doesn't work out, I'll just start all over with someone else."* These things ought not to be so! In the Bible, marriage is not temporary. It is to last for the entire lives of both parties.

Marriage should be something taught by parents to their children as something that is good, wholesome, and morally right. And, it should always be as the vow says, *"Til death do us part."*

I hope in the pages of this work to present exactly what Marriage is according to the BIBLE, and how each party involved is to do his or her part, no matter how hard it may be, in order for a marriage to work according to God's plan. And, I hope the verses presented herein will teach those who are truly seeking how to honor God who founded marriage.

So, let's begin our walk through the Bible and study God's Glorious Institution of this thing we call marriage.

Introduction

Marriage is found in every culture on the face of the earth and can be traced clear back to the very beginning of time. Throughout history men and woman have come together and joined themselves in matrimony and started a family. This was the accepted way of doing things, and it was understood that marriage was what a person needed to do at some time in their life in order to find happiness and fulfill their reason for existence.

But, nowadays, we are seeing a decline in the number of people getting married, and a steady increase in divorces. People today don't want to get married or stay married. They would rather be single. Why is this?

I believe we must first ask this question: *"Why do people get married?"* The answer is that people marry for many different reasons. Some marry because they are lonely, and seek companionship. Others take the plunge because they desire to start a family and preserve their heritage. Then, there are those who get married because they seek security, whether it be money, or a place to live, or a person who will take care of them. But, they all have one thing in common, they all get married because this is what history, family, and their own conscience tells them that they should do.

However, today we live in a society where marriage is downgraded. It's almost as if the world looks at marriage as a curse, or as something that will only *"tie one down."* Modern sinful, promiscuous people want their freedom, and to keep, as they say, *"their options open."* They don't desire to *"tie the knot,"* and settle down with one partner for life in Holy Matrimony. Rather, they want sexual freedom and liberty to fulfill their carnal desires (i.e. fornicate). But, this ought not so to be.

One reason that marriage is so degraded in America is because of what is taught by our secular educational system. In colleges and universities throughout the land, "Evolution" is taught as fact (although there is absolutely no evidence for it), and is pushed upon the students. Because of this, the idea of God (the founder of Marriage), is ridiculed and laughed at; while man is exalted as, *"the measure of all things."*

Man has tried to take over God's position. He has rejected God and His word, and made man's word the final authority.

Secular schools then teach students to believe that Science (falsely so called, according to 1 Tim. 6:20), is fact. Most pupils are taught from an early age that man is nothing more than an animal with the ability to reason, write, and think philosophically. And, if you teach someone that he is an animal long enough, then the logical end would be that he will start living like one! This is exactly what has happened in our country today.

If you study the animal kingdom, you'll see that the animals don't marry one another. However, they do seek a mate, but it's usually not a mate for life, and it's not a marriage relationship. It is copulation for the progeneration of the species, or for just pure enjoyment. The simple fact is that animals don't get married, but people do.

It is very hypocritical for the typical college-educated person who is an atheist or evolutionist to be married, for by the very beliefs he has been taught, he would have to believe that there is no Creator, and that since all men came from animals, that in all actuality, he himself is just an animal. And, as afore mentioned, animals don't get married!

If he did believe that marriage was wholesome, and right, and should be done by all human beings, he would then have to believe that marriage is a man-made idea, and not an institution that God gave to mankind. But, this is of course a tremendous error, as we shall soon see, that must be corrected.

Probably the biggest reason that Marriage is frowned upon by people today, is because God's word is not preached. Truth has fallen in the streets. Far too many Preachers will not stand up and proclaim God's word as it stands, and tell you what it says. They would rather change God's word (with a newer version), or correct it with what they call *"The Greek,"* in order to make it say what they want it to.

But, that precious old King James Bible is what founded America, and the majority of men and women who founded our country were Christians. They were moral people who had a strong belief that the Bible was God's written infallible words, and they followed it as written.

Sadly, today the Bible is frowned upon by "places of higher learning." Instead, the 1960's doctrine of "free love" has penetrated our society and our morals. The motto of men and women today is, *"If it feels good, do it!"* And this of course, will always lead to four things:

fornication, *adultery*, *bastards* and *abortion*. Sadly, this is exactly the society in which we live.

Young men and women of today don't want to get married, and keep the old *"out dated"* family values of their parents. They do whatever they want to do, whenever they want to do it, and don't let anyone tell them any differently. They are rebellious, and wreckless. And, it's all because the Bible, prayer, and the ten commandments have been kicked out of our public schools where our children are enrolled.

Our society has changed from a people that had character, morals, discernment, and a strong work ethic, to a society of young people that live at home, and live for one purpose - to party! And, if a person wants to *"sow their wild oats,"* then Marriage would be a real cramp to their lifestyle.

But, in order to have a moral society, and strong marriages, we must go back to the word of God. As the saying goes, *"Back to the Bible, or Back to the Jungle!"* And, to understand the Institution of Marriage and make it work, one must turn from the world's wisdom, and turn to God to find the answers.

According to the Bible, we clearly see that Marriage was not founded by *man*, but was set up by *God*. The Bible teaches that the idea of Marriage came from the Creator himself, who created both the man and the woman.

When God made male and female, he made them different, and in such a way that they are to supplement one the other. He instilled in them an attraction and a desire one for the other, and made them so that they could join themselves together. He made them so that each one needed the other one. But, with these desires and attractions for each other, God also set up some rules and guidelines for them to follow in order to keep them from becoming promiscuous, and to insure good health, and happiness.

In order to study marriage, one must first accept the fact that God is the one who made man, and that he is the one who told him to marry. One must also accept the Bible, and believe its truths in order to understand God's reasons for giving us the Institution of Matrimony. For it is only in God's book (that God gave man to study) that we can truly understand his reasons for ordaining marriage, and his purposes for it.

Not only must one understand that it was God who instituted marriage, but he must know the very God personally who gave it and set it up in order to understand the Biblical *type* that Marriage is: of Christ and his church.

To truly understand Marriage, one must be born again. Only then can he truly begin to understand this thing called "Holy Matrimony." For not only is it a relationship between a man and a woman, but in type it is a relationship between a born again child of God (a Christian) and his Saviour — Jesus Christ.

Now, let's turn to God's word, and seek His wisdom about this subject, and see for ourselves what God, the Creator, has to say about this God-ordained, God-instituted thing that we call Marriage.

Chapter 1

The Origin of Marriage

As we have seen in the introduction, the origin of marriage was from the very beginning. It was the brainchild of God himself, and not man. God set it up, and instituted it. He then gave man his words about the subject in the Holy Bible, and it's only there that we can find its origin and its reason for being ordained. So, let's look at God's word to see what he says about marriage.

The word *marriage* can be found throughout the pages of the Bible. As we read it, we find the word m*arriage* occurs 19 times in 18 verses in our King James Bible. The word m*arry* appears 19 times in 18 verses, and *married* occurs 30 times in 28 verses in the same version. So, God has much to say about marriage in his word, and we should turn to Him (the founder of it) alone for answers to our questions about it.

Sadly, far too many people today instead turn to Psychologists or Counsellors instead of God for help in their marriage relationship. But, if God instituted marriage, and performed the first ceremony between Adam and Eve, then He would know much more about it than any human Counsellor. Beware of "Counsellors" who say they can help your marriage if they try to give advice or instruction outside of the word of God! The Bible is the only textbook one needs for helping him or her find answers to marital problems.

Not only do we find marriage throughout the entire Bible, but we also find the very first marriage itself. It was performed by God himself between Adam and Eve. (Not Adam and Steve, by the way!)

The Bible tells us in the book of Genesis, chapter 1 and verses 26 and 27, that God created both man and woman.

In Genesis chapter two and verse seven, we read how God did it. And, we also see what he used to create the man. The Bible says:

And the LORD God formed man *of* <u>the dust of the ground</u>, and breathed into his nostrils the breath of life; and man became a living soul.

Then a few verses later we see how God created the woman as well. Read along with me:

Genesis 2:21 And the LORD God caused a deep sleep to fall upon Adam, and he slept: and he took one of his ribs, and closed up the flesh instead thereof;

Genesis 2:22 And the rib, which the LORD God had taken from man, made he a woman, and brought her unto the man.

So, in the beginning, God took one (Adam) and made two (Adam and Eve). But, in the glorious institution of marriage, God takes two, and makes one. What a marvelous and awesome thing this is!

God confirms this blessed union of two becoming one as we read on:

Genesis 2:23 And Adam said, This is now bone of my bones, and flesh of my flesh: she shall be called Woman, because she was taken out of Man.

Genesis 2:24 Therefore shall a man leave his father and his mother, and shall cleave unto his wife: and they shall be one flesh.

This was God's plan for marriage from the beginning and has always been throughout history. It's God's desire that *one man* and *one woman* come together in Holy Matrimony as *one flesh* for the remainder of their lives.

From the Bible we clearly see that marriage is something that God has ordained and instituted. And, we can conclude that in order for a marriage to work, it is something that must be based upon God's holy word. For he is the one who designed it.

When you buy a new car and look in the glovebox, you will find an Owner's Manual. It tells you where the car came from, who made it, and how to fix it if it breaks. It is the same with God's word. It is our Instruction Manual, not only in all areas of life, but also in the glorious Institution of Marriage as well.

Now, let's begin studying more in-depth about the creation of both the man and woman in light of the scriptures, and what God says about them.

Why The Man was Created

To understand Marriage, one needs to understand why both the man and the woman were created. This will help to understand the purposes of both genders, and why God made them the way they are. We'll start with Adam.

The Bible plainly tells us that Adam was created in *God's image* (Genesis 1:27), and God made him like himself. He was created a tripartite being, just like God. Look at what God says in Genesis 1:26,

And God said, Let us make man in our image, after our likeness: and let them have dominion over the fish of the sea, and over the fowl of the air, and over the cattle, and over all the earth, and over every creeping thing that creepeth upon the earth.

God is talking to himself when he says this and he says to himself, "**Let us make man in our image**..." God refers to himself in the plural, and there is a reason for this. God is a *Trinity*. He is one God with three parts. And, just like God has three parts, so does man. In Thessalonians 5:23 Paul tells us exactly what these three parts are. We read, "**And the very God of peace sanctify you wholly; and *I pray God* your whole spirit and soul and body be preserved blameless unto the coming of our Lord Jesus Christ.**"

So, the three parts of a man are his *spirit, soul,* and *body.* God has these three parts as well. They are the Holy Ghost (the spirit), God the Father (the soul), and Jesus Christ the Son (the body). God is a Trinity. And man is also a tri-part being, who was originally made in God's image.

But, you know the rest of the story. In Genesis chapter three, and verse six, we find Adam falling from his created state. Adam sinned against God, and he fell. He was no longer sinless. He became a Sinner.

The Bible goes on to tell us in Genesis 5:3, that all men born after Adam are born in *Adam's image* (not God's). Thus, Adam became a sinful man, and he passed his sin nature to all men (Romans 5:12). And, the Bible tells us that all men today are Sinners in need of a new birth (John 3:3,7). They <u>must</u> be born again in order to be like Adam was before he fell.

Thus far, we have seen a little more about the man, and how he was originally created in God's image. But now let us turn our attention to the reasons *why* man was created.

The first reason was to *PRAISE* and worship God. In Revelation 4:8 we find there are some beings around the throne of God. The Bible says it is their job to give God glory and honor day and night as they continually repeat, "**Holy, holy, holy, Lord God Almighty, which was, and is, and is to come**." (And, I say unto you that God deserves every "Holy" ever said! All eternity won't be long enough to tell God how holy he really is! He is an awesome God!)

Now, these beings, were made for one purpose and one purpose only—to *praise* God. And, they did it because they had to. They were made to do just that. It was the only reason they were created. But, God wanted someone to worship him, and honor him, and praise him because they wanted to — not because it was required. This is real love. It is loving someone because you *want* to, and not because you *have* to. So, God made man, and gave him a freewill in order to choose whether or not he wanted to praise, honor, and obey God. And, when man did it because he wanted to, and not because he had to, it honored God the more. This made God happy.

Another reason that God made man can be found in Rev. 4:11. It states:

Thou art worthy, O Lord, to receive glory and honour and power: for thou hast created all things, and <u>for thy pleasure</u> they are and were created.

Man was created to *PLEASE* God. For centuries men have been asking the philosophical question, "*Why are we here?*" They ask, "*What is our reason for existence?*" They spend hours searching libraries full of books. They listen to great speakers and "men of renown." They write volumes on their theories, opinions, and ideas about the subject.

But, the answer is found only in the Bible, and is so simple, that it's hard to believe that they could have missed it. The answer is only three words long! According to the Bible, man was created, "***For His pleasure***." Man's purpose for being is to *please* God.

But, today sinful mankind is not interested in pleasing God at all. They only want to please themselves. How sad this is. And, how disappointed God must be with man. For, mankind is not fulfilling his reason for existence. How tired God must be of putting up with sinful man, who has forgotten his Maker, and only cares about *pleasuring himself.*

Finally, God made man to *POPULATE* the earth. Not only did God want one man (Adam) to praise and please him. He wanted all of mankind to do so. So, in Gen. 1:28 he said to Adam, "...**Be fruitful, and multiply, and replenish the earth**..."

God wanted a whole planet filled with people that would want to worship and honor him freely of their own freewill. But, this population could not take place without the woman. So, let's look at her next, and her reason for being created.

Why Woman was Created

Before Adam sinned, God saw that he was alone physically. So, God decided to give him a companion. And, that's exactly what God did when he made woman.

The reason God gives in the Bible for making woman, and yea even ordaining Marriage was for the man's sake.

Read with me in Genesis 2:18:

And the LORD God said, *It is* **not good that the man should be alone; I will make him and help meet for him.**

God said that Adam was alone. And, it was *not good*. So God made someone for him, that would be with him, and be a *help* to him. She was to *meet* his needs.

Paul testifies to this as well in 1 Corinthians 11:9, which states:

Neither was the man created for the woman; but the woman for the man.

So, we see that God made man for himself, and then God made woman for the man. The man was to please God, and the woman was to please the man.

Now, you must understand, Eve was not created to help Adam *spiritually*. He had perfect fellowship with God. He walked with God on a daily basis, and talked with him. No, Eve was made to help Adam's *physical needs*.

In Ecclessiastes 4:9-11, we glean some of the reasons why God made woman for man. There we read:

vs 9 Two *are* better than one; because they have a good reward for their labour.

vs 10 For if they fall, the one will lift up his fellow: but woe to him *that is* alone when he falleth; for *he hath* not another to help him up.

vs 11 Again, if two lie together, then they have heat: but how can one be warm *alone?*

God saw the great need the man had for some things. He saw that he needed someone to give him heat at night. He saw that two could work together better than one, and get twice as much done. He saw that if one fell the other could lift him or her up. And, on and on. But above all this, God saw man's loneliness, and desire for companionship. And, it was for these reasons that God made woman. She was created for Adam's benefit.

I'm sure Adam saw all the animals in pairs walking two by two, frolicking around and playfully biting and chasing one another. And, I'm sure Adam began to wonder where there was another like himself. Someone he could have fun with, and spend time with. And, God in his omnipotence knew Adam's desire for a friend, a companion, and a mate. So, God caused a deep sleep to fall upon Adam, and then he made Mrs. Adam as a *help*, meet for his needs. God made Adam a fellow human being of opposite gender to be with and to love. She was to be his friend, companion, helper, lover, and mate. And, this is just what a woman should be to her husband today. She needs to realize that she was made for him, to be a help to him.

As afore mentioned, we read that the woman came from the man (she was taken from his side). But, nowadays, the man comes from the woman. Herein is a great irony: the first woman came from a man (Adam), and all other men come from a woman (their mother) through childbirth. Paul says this in 1 Corinthians. 11:12 as he states:

For as the woman *is* of the man [Adam], even so *is* the man also by the woman [Eve]; but all things of God.

So, according to the Bible, the woman was created to marry one man, and be a help to him and meet his needs. This is her purpose and reason for being created. And, a woman will never be happy until she is in her God-called role, fulfilling God's word and his plan for her life.

It is interesting to note that in the Bible, the woman has no name of her own. God never called the woman

"Eve." It was Adam that called her name *Eve* (Gen. 3:20) But, in Genesis 5:2, God called them both Adam. Why? Because in God's eyes they were *married*. They were one flesh. And, a woman's purpose and very reason for being created was for marriage. She was made to fit the man, to complete him, and to be a helper to him.

Today when a woman is born, she too has no last name of her own. At birth, she's given her father's last name. Then when she is married, she takes her husband's last name. This is to remind her of her origin (she came from man) and her purpose. She was created as Paul so amply puts it, "**for the man**."

Finally, we find in Genesis not only the origin of man and woman, but also the origin of marriage. The first marriage was performed in the Garden of Eden. What better place is there to have a wedding than in a garden? Because of this, people still want flowers at their weddings today!

So, in conclusion, we must remember God made man for his pleasure to *please him*, to *praise him*, and to *populate the earth*. Then God made woman for the man to help him accomplish this task. And, right there in that beautiful, colorful paradise called "the Garden of Eden," God took the two and made one. And, this "one" was a blessed union in the eyes of God.

So, this brings to a close our study of the origin of marriage and of the man and woman. Let's continue with the next chapter on what Marriage is, according to the Bible.

Chapter 2

What Marriage is

A Joining

The Bible says that marriage is several things. Let's first look at what Jesus Christ said about it in Matthew 19:4-6:

> **4 And he answered and said unto them, Have ye not read, that he which made them at the beginning made them male and female,**
>
> **5 And said, For this cause shall a man leave father and mother, and shall cleave to his wife: and they twain shall be one flesh?**
>
> **6 Wherefore they are no more twain, but one flesh. What therefore God hath <u>joined</u> together, let not man put asunder.**

And, we see almost the identical statement from Jesus Christ again in Mark 10:6-9:

6 But from the beginning of the creation God made them male and female.

7 For this cause shall a man leave his father and mother, and cleave to his wife;

8 And they twain shall be one flesh: so then they are no more twain, but one flesh.

9 What therefore God hath <u>joined</u> together, let not man put asunder.

According to the above verses, marriage is a *joining together* of two people of opposite genders before God. And, it is to be until death. God says that neither party is to put it asunder. (That is they should never get divorced).

This joining together that the scripture speaks of here is the flesh of the man joining the flesh of the woman. In marriage, we call this the "consummation." But, just because *flesh joins flesh* in a sexual act, doesn't always mean you have a marriage. Look at these verses again. In Mark 10:9 we read the important words, "**What <u>God hath joined</u> together, let not man put asunder**."

The Bible says that *God* has a part in this joining as well. So, in order for it to be a marriage, God must approve of the "consummation," or joining of the two people sexually. If God does not approve, then it is not marriage. It is *fornication* or *adultery*.

Now to understand this, we need to look at the Bible definition of marriage. It is found in Hebrews 13:4. It states:

Marriage *is* honourable in all, and the bed undefiled: but whoremongers and adulterers God will judge.

The Bible says that marriage is two things: *honourable* and *undefiled*.

So, if it is to be a marriage according to the Scriptural definition, the joining of flesh with flesh must be *honorable* in God's eyes and *without defilement*. If it is not honorable, then it's not a marriage according to this definition.

The *honor* in this verse has to do with the man and the woman honoring God (who instituted Marriage), and honoring each other. And, people need to do that in order to have a real marriage.

Some claim that all flesh joining flesh constitutes a marriage. But this is not the case. For if we are to believe that all flesh on flesh is marriage, then we must believe that *RAPE* is marriage as it joins two bodies together. We must also believe that *HOMOSEXUALITY* is marriage for they join themselves together. We must further believe that *FORNICATION* is marriage. And, we must also accept that *BEASTIALITY* is marriage. But, common sense (as well as the Bible) tells us this is not so. God must have a part in the joining as we have seen in the verses from Matthew and Mark. It must be an honorable joining of the flesh to be marriage in God's sight.

This is why for thousands of years people have gone to churches or synagogues to be wed. It was to join themselves together in "Holy Matrimony" before God, and to honor him in their wedding vows. This is the only way flesh joining flesh can be done *honorably*.

The Bible calls sexual intercourse outside of Marriage "Fornication," and the Bible commands us to flee from that in 1 Corinthians. 6:18.

There are many in this world today who are fornicators, they have joined their bodies to someone else, but are they in the site of God married, because they did so? The Biblical answer is "No," because it was dishonorably done, and defiling.

Let's look at some more Bible examples that prove that flesh joining flesh is not always a marriage. It must have God's stamp of approval on it, and he must be honored in it for it to be so.

God says in the scriptures that rape is not a marriage even though it is flesh on flesh. In Genesis chapter 34, we read about a man named Shechem who raped Dinah the daughter of Jacob (Israel). Now, look at verse 2:

And when Shechem the son of Hamor the Hivite, prince of the country, saw her, he took her, and lay with her, and <u>defiled her</u>.

Then in verse 4, we read, "**And Shechem spake unto his father Hamor, saying, Get me this damsel to wife.**"

So, according to the scriptures, they were <u>not</u> married. Why? Because she was *defiled* by his act of raping her. And, the Bible says that after the flesh joined flesh, *then* Shechem wanted to *marry* her.

Dinah was "**defiled**." And, because of this defilement, the Bible clearly tells us that they were not married. The act was dishonorable in God's eyes. And, God was not honored in it, nor did he condone it.

Not only is rape not a marriage, but the Bible teaches that Homosexual acts of joining are not marriage either. Let's look at this in the following verses:

Leviticus 18:22 Thou shalt not lie with mankind, as with womankind: <u>it *is* abomination</u>.

Leviticus 18:23 Neither shalt thou lie with any beast to defile thyself therewith: neither shall any woman stand before a beast to lie down thereto: it *is* confusion.

Leviticus 18:24 Defile not ye yourselves in any of these things: for in all these the nations are defiled which I cast out before you:

Leviticus 18:25 And <u>the land is defiled</u>: therefore I do visit the iniquity thereof upon it, and the land itself vomiteth out her inhabitants.

According to these verses, God says that homosexuality is a sin, and it is *defiling* to those that participate in it. *Beastiality* is also said to be a defilement, and God says that these sins not only *defile* those doing them, but also the land in which they live.

So, we see that homosexual acts and beastiality are not marriage in God's eyes, even though they join flesh together.

The Bible also says that adultery is not a marriage even though it too joins flesh with flesh. A good example to prove this is found in Luke 3:19, the Bible says:

But Herod the tetrarch, being reproved by him for Herodias <u>his brother Philip's wife</u>, and for all the evils which Herod had done.

We find in this verse two people together named Herod and Herodias. And, in the context of the passage, John the Baptist is preaching against their adulterous relationship of being together.

Undoubtedly, they were engaged in sexual relations. And, if we are to believe that every time flesh joins flesh it constitutes a marriage, then we must believe that Herod and Herodias were indeed married. But, according to John the Baptist who preached against their adulterous affair, and God the Holy Spirit who penned the words **"his brother Philip's wife**," this was not the case. As far as God was concerned, Herodias was Philip's wife, and not Herod's. Why? Because Herod and Herodius' flesh had been joined dishonorably in the act of *adultery*.

But, we can't leave out the verse in Mark 6:17 either. We read later that Herod "**married her**." This shows that Herod did want to make a dishonorable thing honorable, and he tried to do so. Probably he was under conviction by the preaching of John the Baptist, and wanted to get right. So he most likely went to a temple and exchanged wedding vows with Herodias.

But, according to the scriptures, God still called her Philip's wife because that is who she should have been with in God's eyes. Herod and Herodias' relationship was one of adultery. And, the definition of adultery is: *"two things coming together that don't belong together."*

Thus, God looks at joinings of the flesh to see whether or not they are done *honorably* or *dishonorably*. If it is not right, then God does not accept it as marriage.

Let's look at one other case. In 2 Samuel 11:1-4, the Bible says that David saw Bathsheba and lusted after her, and then he sent messengers to go get her. Then in vs 4 we read:

and [he] took her; and she came in unto him, and he lay with her; for she was purified from her uncleanness: and she returned unto her house.

This was flesh joining flesh. It was a sexual encounter between the two. But, look at what the Holy Spirit says in verse 26:

And when the <u>wife of Uriah</u> heard that Uriah her husband was dead, she mourned for her husband.

God says that Bathsheba was still Uriah's wife, even after David's flesh had joined with her flesh. And, David the adulterer was judged according to Hebrews 13:4. He had to pay four fold for killing Uriah, and committing adultery (2 Sam. 12:9).

Then in 2 Sam. 11:24, we read these words:

And when the mourning was past, David sent and fetched her to his house, and <u>she became his wife</u>, and bare him a son. <u>But the thing that David had done displeased the LORD</u>.

David and Bathsheba were later married (joined honorably before God) after Uriah death. But, their sin of adultery before they were married greatly displeased the Lord.

Now let's close with what Paul says about fornication in 1 Corinthians chapter six, and verse thirteen. We read, "..**Now the body *is* not for fornication, but for the Lord; and the Lord for the body**." God does not want a man or a woman to fornicate (join flesh with flesh before marriage). God wants the joining to be done honorably within the bounds of the marriage relationship. He wants it to be honorable, and he wants to be honored in it.

God does not want a man to join his flesh dishonorably in either *adultery* or *fornication*. Nor does he want man to join himself with a harlot. Let's look at what Paul says about this in the following verses:

1 Corinthians 6:15 Know ye not that your bodies are the members of Christ? shall I then take the members of Christ, and make them the members of an harlot? God forbid.

1 Corinthians 6:16 What? know ye not that he which is joined to an harlot is one body? for two, saith he, shall be one flesh.

1 Corinthians 6:17 But he that is joined unto the Lord is one spirit.

1 Corinthians 6:18 Flee fornication. Every sin that a man doeth is without the body; but he that committeth fornication sinneth against his own body.

Paul, here, is making a contrast in these verses between a man joining himself together with a *harlot* (something that's dishonorable), and the members of Christ joining themselves to God (something that's honorable).

Paul tells us that a man who sleeps with a harlot is *ONE FLESH* with that harlot. This raises the question: *"Is it possible to join one's flesh to another and become ONE FLESH with them, and still not be married to them?"*

Well, in this passage of scripture, Paul asks Christians if *he* should join them to a harlot, and, his answer is **"God forbid"** that should happen! Then he tells them in verse 16, that when two join themselves together, they do become *one flesh*. (That is when they are *joined* in the act, they are one).

But, notice Paul does not say they have become *married*. Why? because the joining together in one flesh in whoredom is the act of fornication, and this is the context (vs 13). Paul is using this as an illustration to tell them that they are one with Christ, and not one with a harlot.

The question still remains: *"Is it possible for two to become one flesh, and still not be married?"* If we stick with our definition of marriage in Hebrews 13:4, then it is possible. A man can become "one flesh" with a harlot, and still not be married to her. For his joining of his flesh to that harlot would be *dishonorable*, and *defiling*. According to the Bible, marriage is *"honorable,"* and *"undefiled."*

Thus, there are two kinds of joining sexually—an *honorable joining* and a *dishonorable joining*. If it is done dishonorably, according to Hebrews 13:4, it is not marriage. It is either *fornication* or *adultery*. Whoredom is not marriage.

As we have seen, marriage has to do with flesh on flesh, but only when that fleshly joining is undefiled and honorable in the eyes of God. If it is dishonorable, or defiled, then it is most certainly not a marriage, it is fornication or adultery.

So what makes joining flesh honorable in the eyes of God? The answer is simple. The two parties must be in agreement that they are joining themselves together according to God's word, with the purpose of following God's plan for marriage in their lives. That of course, would be a covenant that they make one to the other to stay together for life, and only be faithful to their mate.

Commitment vs Covenant

It has been said by some that marriage is just a *commitment* between two people. But is this so? According to the Bible, it is more than a commitment, it is a *covenant.*

Let's first look at the difference between a covenant and a commitment, for marriage is much more than just a commitment, although that is a part of it. A *commitment* is when you make up your mind to commit to someone or something. But, a *covenant* is when you sware allegiance to something, with no possibility of going against it.

When a man and woman make a commitment, they tell the other person that they will willingly put themselves in a situation of allowing that other person to know that they are for them or with them. But, a commitment can be broken with no legal binding. A covenant however is a little different.

A covenant is when you sware an oath or make a vow to someone. And, it is binding. In marriage, not only does a person make a solemn vow to their partner for life, that they are to honor, but they also are making this vow before God. And, God takes these vows very seriously, even if those making them don't. We will see more about this vow in the next section. But, first let's look at what God says about marriage being a covenant in the Bible.

In Ezekiel 16:8, God is speaking to Israel about Marriage. And, he says the following:

Now when I passed by thee, and looked upon thee, behold, thy time *was* **the time of love; and I spread my skirt over thee, and covered thy nakedness: yea, I <u>sware unto thee, and entered into a covenant with thee</u>, saith the Lord GOD, and thou becamest mine.**

God says he spread his skirt over Israel (this would be a type of the consummation of the marriage). But, look at the rest of the verse. God said that he entered into a *covenant* with her as well, and a vow (*I sware unto thee*). And, when this vow is made, then they are husband and wife as far as God is concerned.

So, marriage has to do with the flesh joining flesh, but it must be honorable, and for it to be honorable, both must make a covenant with each other, and sware to stay together. The Marriage Vow binds them one to another before God, and the consummation joins the two together as one body (one flesh).

Let's look at Mary and Joseph as an example of this. In Luke 1:27 we read about Mary as a virgin, who is **"espoused to a man whose name was Joseph."** The word *espouse* means *to promise or engage in marriage, by contract in writing, or by some pledge; promised in marriage*. That is, there is a *promise* (a vow), and an intention of marriage is involved.

But in Luke 2:5 we find the Holy Spirit calling Mary, Joseph's **wife** *BEFORE* they are even wed. How can this be? How can God call Mary Joseph's wife before they have joined together in consummation?

If flesh on flesh is all that makes a marriage, then Joseph must have had sex with Mary at this time. But, we know that this is not so. He did not have intercourse with her until after she gave birth to Jesus. The Bible is very clear about this, and confirms this in Matthew 1:25. It says "**he [Joseph] knew her not til she brought forth her firstborn son.**"

So, there was no consummation there, but God looked at them as though they were married. How could this be? We must turn to the scriptures for the answer.

Read with me if you will, the following verses:

Mat 1:18 Now the birth of Jesus Christ was on this wise: When as his mother Mary was espoused to Joseph, before they came together, she was found with child of the Holy Ghost.

Mat 1:19 Then Joseph her husband, being a just man, and not willing to make her a public example, was minded to put her away privily.

Mat 1:20 But while he thought on these things, behold, the angel of the Lord appeared unto him in a dream, saying, Joseph, thou son of David, fear not to take unto thee Mary thy wife: for that which is conceived in her is of the Holy Ghost.

According to these verses, Mary was espoused (promised) to Joseph to be his wife, but they were not yet married. When Mary became pregnant, Joseph thought about putting her away, because he thought she had committed fornication with another man and that's why she was pregnant. But, God told him not to do so, and to take her and marry her.

Then we read these words:

Mat 1:24 Then Joseph being raised from sleep did as the angel of the Lord had bidden him, and took unto him his wife:

So, there is more to marriage than just the aspect of flesh meeting flesh. That joins the bodies, but the covenant or vow joins them together by a bond or a promise to God. And, this is what God is looking for.

God was looking at Joseph's heart, and saw that he had made up his mind to stay with Mary no matter what, and as far as God was concerned, they were married when Joseph took her unto him with the determination in his heart to take care of her, and stay with her till death.

There was no flesh that joined flesh yet, but as far as God was concerned, they were husband and wife. Why is this? Because they made a decision to stay with each other, and this was recognizable in the eyes of God.

God, therefore, looks at the motive of the two people coming together, whether or not they are coming together before him to honor him, or whether or not they are coming together just to fulfill the carnal desires of the flesh. And, this motive is what determines whether or not the consummation is honorable or dishonorable.

We must realize that there is more to marriage than just flesh on flesh. Yes, that's what joins husband and wife together physically as one. But, there is another aspect to it as well, and that is *the reason* why they are joining themselves together. Is it to honor God, and consummate their vow to stay together for life, or is it just to have a good time? The motive must be to honor God. And, this is what God looks for.

Thus, the only way to understand the preceding verses, is to understand that God only counts it as a marriage, if the two come together before God, and bind themselves one to the other with a covenant or a vow to join themselves together, and stay together until death. This is the essence of marriage.

The Vow

As we learned from the preceding paragraphs, there is more to Marriage than just the act of flesh joining flesh. It must have God's approval, and it must honor him, and then and only then comes the joining of flesh on flesh. If this does not take place, then as far as God is concerned, it is fornication, or adultery. The *joining* must be honorable to be accepted by God. There must be a covenant between the two parties honoring God and his institution of holy matrimony.

But then there are those that go to the opposite extreme and say that Marriage has nothing at all to do with the flesh on flesh aspect, and it is just two people that love each other coming together and signing a piece of paper. But, this too is erroneous, as it leaves God out.

Marriage is more than just signing a piece of paper. We call that the *Marriage Contract* or *Marriage License*. But, marriage, as we have seen, is more than just that. It is a *binding* of each other to God and themselves by a covenant. And, this binding is by what we call "The Wedding Vows."

Once again, let's look at the Bible definition of Marriage. Hebrews 13:4 states:

Marriage *is* honourable in all, and the bed undefiled: but whoremongers and adulterers God will judge.

Marriage is *honourable* according to the Bible. That means there is some honor involved. That honor has to do with honoring God (who instituted marriage), and honoring each other. And, people need to do that in order to have a marriage.

I've seen many people just go down to the courthouse to get married. But, they have left out the most important person—God! And, he needs to be honored in the marriage, as He is the one who instituted it.

Let's look at the definition of Marriage in the 1828 Webster's dictionary. There it is defined as:

The act of uniting a man and woman for life; wedlock; the legal union of a man and woman for life. Marriage is a contract both civil and religious, by which the parties engage to live together in mutual affection and fidelity, till death shall separate them. Marriage was instituted by God himself for the purpose of preventing the promiscuous intercourse of the sexes, for promoting domestic felicity, and for securing the maintenance and education of children.

So, according to this definition, marriage is both *civil* and *religious*. It must be recognized by God, as well as by man. If God is left out, and all you have is flesh joining flesh, then that is only fornication. And, if man does not recognize it, then there will be much promiscuity, infidelity, and unfaithfulness. God must be honored, and man must know that the two are bound together by a promise to be faithful to one another. There must be a *convenant* (made to God and each other) and a *contract* (a legal document showing man that the two are wed).

But, people today don't look at marriage that way. How sad this is. Yet, the truth still remains: Marriage is two people coming together before God and making a vow to be faithful only to one another and stay with one another "as long as they both shall live!"

If only people today would approach marriage this way! Instead of the right Biblical attitude of *"No matter what, I'll stick with this person,"* their thinking is, *"Well, if it doesn't work out, I'll just find someone else."* That's not right! That's not biblical! That's not marriage! That is nothing but pure selfishness! And, a person with that attitude will not stay married very long, and will usually end up breaking their vow to their spouse and to God, while seeking divorce papers to undo their civil contract. People who do such as this blaspheme God's word, and His plan for marriage.

Thus, we must understand that in the Bible, marriage is a covenant, which consists of making a vow to your mate and to God that you will stay with that person until death do you part! And, God takes these vows very seriously, even if those making them don't.

Notice with me if you will, what God said in Numbers chapter 30 and verse 2:

If a man vow a vow unto the LORD, or swear an oath to bind his soul with a bond; he shall

not break his word, he shall do according to all that proceedeth out of his mouth.

God believes that a vow is an important thing to follow through with. He even says in this verse that it binds a person's *soul*. It puts the person in *bondage* to his vow. That's how important a vow is.

God also says that it's sin not to follow through with a vow. Look at Deuteronomy 23:21. It says, "**When thou shalt vow a vow unto the LORD thy God, thou shalt not slack to pay it: for the LORD thy God will surely require it of thee; and it would be sin in thee.**" The Bible says it's a *SIN* unto God to break your marriage vows!

Also look at Ecclesiastes 5:4. It reads, "**When thou vowest a vow unto God, defer not to pay it; for he hath no pleasure in fools: pay that which thou hast vowed.**" Here, God calls a person a *FOOL* who breaks their vows.

God is dogmatic about keeping your vows. Ecclesiastes 5:5 says, "**Better *is it* that thou shouldest not vow, than that thou shouldest vow and not pay.**"

Thus, the Bible is very clear on this matter. Marriage is a man and a woman coming together before God and making a vow to stay together as one flesh. They are to abide by these vows, and continue together throughout their lives as husband and wife.

God hates divorce! He hates it when a person goes against his or her vows. He calls it *sin*, and the person that does it he calls a *fool* (Ecclesiastes 5:4). God's intention for marriage was (and still is) for two people to get married and stay together for life.

Anyone who gets married and then divorces his or her mate has then gone against God's word, and their own word. And, according to the Bible, they are a *promise breaker*, a *liar*, and *dishonorable* in the eyes of a holy God.

A person is only as good as his or her word. And, it is better for a person not to sware or vow an oath to stay with someone, than to sware it and not follow through with it. For to break one's vow, means that a person will give account to God someday for it.

Thank God that when God swears something or vows something to man, it is sure that he will follow through with it! We can trust wholly and completely upon Him, and His precious promises! But, how can a person trust his or her spouse if they are not putting God's word first in their lives?

We need to realize that for a marriage to work, and to keep it from ending in sin (divorce), we must look to and obey God's word for the rules and guidelines to go by for a successful marriage. Then, and only then will we understand marriage, and be able to honor God.

Chapter 3

Why Marriage was Instituted

The Bible is very clear on the origin of Marriage. It originated in the Garden of Eden, and was ordained to honor God. It started with Adam and Eve. It was between one man and one woman, and was meant to be for life. But, the question needs be asked, *"Why did God institute it?"*

There are many answers to this question. We shall look at only a few below:

For Fellowship

First, marriage was set up for a man to have *fellowship* with his wife. Adam had a spiritual relationship with God in the Garden of Eden. But, he had no one like him, whom he could have as a friend. He wanted someone to be with, and to do things with. Someone like himself, whose company he could enjoy.

It is a known fact that all people need love. And, a man needs love just as much as a woman (if not more). And, a person who is lonely will usually end up in depression, discouragement, or distress. Everyone needs someone to fellowship with, and to talk too. And, this is one reason that God made woman for the man. He needed physical fellowship with a mate, as well as spiritual fellowship with God.

For Fruit

God also made the woman for the man to help him start a *family*. And, the woman is able to give him children. She is the *Womb man*. She was made with the ability to bring life into this world. It is the man's seed, and therefore technically his child, but it's the woman's blood, sweat, and tears that take care of that child as it grows into adulthood. She cares for it and loves it. She feeds it, and teaches it how to mature. She nurtures it with sweet tender loving care. Yes, there is nothing in this world like the love of a mother, (except of course the love of God the Father).

When it comes to children in the marriage relationship, both the man and woman have responsibilities. They each need to be likeminded and raise that child for the glory of God, and teach it what marriage is. Otherwise the Institution of Marriage will fall apart as time goes by, and society as a whole will crumble. A nation will never be any better than the homes in that nation, and a church will only be as spiritual as those families in that local assembly.

So childbearing and childrearing ought to be looked upon as an awesome responsibility. Those blessed children that a husband and wife produce are the fruit of their love one for another, and are a gift from God. And, it's God's desire for husband and wife not only to produce that fruit, but then to teach that child, and instruct him from God's word to help him grow spiritually.

Once again let's read the command that God gave to Adam and Eve in Genesis 1:28:

"And God blessed them, and God said unto them, Be fruitful, and multiply, and replenish the earth."

So, God definitely gave the Institution of Marriage to bring forth children in wedlock that would be taken care of and protected by their parents. Nobody will love and protect and take care of that child better than its parents.

And, according to God's plan, a child should be trained up in the nurture and admonition of the Lord, and instructed by its parents on how to have a good marriage as well.

For Faithfulness

The final reason, and probably the greatest, that God instituted marriage was so that a man and woman would be *faithful* one to another and stay together. It was to keep them from being like the animals and going around mating with many different partners. It was to teach them to love each other, and be faithful one to another.

If there were no marriage, then promiscuity would have run rampant throughout the ages and sexually transmitted diseases would be common. But, fidelity keeps this from happening. If there were no marriage, then many illegitimate children would abound, and society would crumble as the family unit would cease to exist. God in his infinite wisdom wanted to keep this from happening.

In 1 Corinthians 7 and verse 2, we read, "**Nevertheless, *to avoid* fornication, let every man have his own wife, and let every woman have her own husband.**"

God set up marriage to avoid fornication. As you probably know, God instilled in everyone a sex drive, in order to ensure the preservation of the species. And, this God-given desire for the opposite sex, was intended to be fulfilled, but not in fornication! God wanted it done decently and honorably between two people that love each other and have promised to be faithful one to another. Notice yet again the definition of Marriage in Hebrews 13:4,

Marriage *is* honourable in all, and <u>the bed undefiled</u>: but whoremongers and adulterers God will judge.

God says in marriage, that the bed is undefiled. It is honorable for a husband and wife to meet each other's needs sexually in the bedroom. And, God is adamant about this desire being fulfilled in the right manner. In 1 Corinthians 7:9, God says it's better to "**marry than to burn**." This of course refers to burning in your lusts.

One reason God instituted marriage was so a man or woman would marry and have one partner to meet their sexual needs, in order to keep them from the temptation of the flesh to fornicate with many different partners. God wanted them to have only one mate. For, more than one is dishonorable, and leads to whoredoms.

The Bible says that the marriage bed between one man and one woman is honorable and undefiled, but the bed of an Harlot or the Bed of Fornication is not. Let's look at some examples of this.

A good place to study marriage is Deuteronomy chapter 22 verses 22-29. But, let's look at vs 22 first. It says:

If a man be found lying with a woman married to an husband, then they shall both of them die, *both* the man that lay with the woman, and the woman: so shalt thou put away evil from Israel.

This of course would be adultery as spoken of in Hebrews 13:4, and God's judgment in the Old Testament for those found guilty was to be stoned to death. (Boy, if we practiced this today, there would be far less adultery!)

Then in Deuteronomy 22:23-24 we see almost the same thing, but we also learn something interesting. Look at these verses carefully:

Deuteronomy 22:23 If a damsel that is a virgin be betrothed unto an husband, and a man find her in the city, and lie with her;

Deuteronomy 22:24 Then ye shall bring them both out unto the gate of that city, and ye shall stone them with stones that they die; the damsel, because she cried not, *being* in the city; and the man, because he hath humbled his neighbour's wife: so thou shalt put away evil from among you.

These verses are again talking about adultery, but they do show us something important. God talks about the betrothal of a man and woman. *Betroth* means *to contract to anyone, in order to a future marriage, to promise or pledge one to be the future spouse of another.* It is a promise. And, God calls a woman who is betrothed to a man "her husband," and He calls her his "wife." So, what it's saying is that God looks at the promise (not only the vow) as binding even before the flesh of the husband and wife join each other. And, if she joins herself to another man while *betrothed* to another man, then it is adultery in God's eyes. She is to keep herself pure while waiting for her husband.

This shows us once again that God is looking at the heart of a man, and whether or not his intent is to follow through with his promise, and honor God by following through with the vows he is going to make. God looks to see if He is honored in the union or *joining* for it to be marriage.

Look also at these next two verses:

Deuteronomy 22:28 If a man find a damsel that is a virgin, which is not betrothed, and lay hold on her, and lie with her, and they be found;

Deuteronomy 22:29 Then the man that lay with her shall <u>give unto the damsel's father fifty *shekels* of silver</u>, and <u>she shall be his wife</u>; because he hath humbled her, he may not put her away all his days.

Just because the man in this passage joined his flesh with that of the woman, doesn't mean he married her. He took advantage of her, he humbled her, and he defiled her the Bible says in an act of fornication. But, he did not marry her.

But, if he comes back later and gives her father money (what we call a dowry) then she and he are married. Why? because he shows God that he wants to and is willing to do the right thing in marrying her and taking care of her. And, according to the law, the dowry is his promise to do just that. He is to stay with her till death, and "**not put her away all his days**." That is the honorable thing to do according to God. It is the only way to turn a dishonorable joining into an honorable enterprise.

In Exodus 22:16 and 17 we see almost the same scenario.

> **Exodus 22:16 And if a man entice a maid that is not betrothed, and lie with her, he shall surely endow her to be his wife.**

> **Exodus 22:17 If her father utterly refuse to give her unto him, he shall pay money according to the dowry of virgins.**

The man in this verse has lain with a woman, and God says he <u>must</u> "**endow her to be his wife**." The word *endow* here means *to settle a dower on a woman, to furnish with a gift, to settle on*. He must marry her because he defiled her. And, in order to do so, he must pay a dowry to the father. It must cost him something for his sin of fornication. And, he must needs stay with the woman and vow to never put her away (Deuteronomy 22:29).

So, in closing of this chapter, let me say again that God set up the institution of Marriage for several reasons. It was so that a man and a wife could have *fellowship* one with another physically, and with God spiritually (and a threefold cord is not quickly broken - Ecclesiastes

4:12). It also was instituted to bring forth *fruit*, to set up a family unit, and to *keep society from falling to pieces*.

But, most importantly marriage was set up to keep men and woman from committing fornication, and having promiscuous sex before or after marriage. This leads to diseases, heartaches, jealousies, murder, and if unchecked, homosexuality and even beastiality. And, these things dishonor and displease God greatly!

Chapter 4

The Order of Marriage

As we have already seen, God made the man first. Then he created the woman. And, the woman was created to help the man. So, the man obviously was already busy doing some things.

Genesis 2:20 tells us the following:

And Adam gave names to all cattle, and to the fowl of the air, and to every beast of the field; but for Adam there was not found an help meet for him.

While Adam was busy naming the animals, God saw that he needed a helper. Adam must have seen that all the animals had another kind opposite of themselves. And, Adam must have wondered, *"Where is mine?" "Where is a female of my species?"* So, God made a woman for him.

In Genesis 2:15, we see another one of Adam's duties.

And the LORD God took the man, and put him into the garden of Eden to dress it and to keep it.

Adam's job was to keep the garden. But, how hard was that? All he had to do was pick the fruit and eat it. Adam had it *"made in the shade,"* as we say. He really didn't have to do much.

According to Genesis 1:26, Adam had dominion over the fish, the fowl, and the cattle as well. But, what did he have to do for them except name them, and he did that himself in vs. 20. So, the jobs that Adam had to do looked pretty easy. And, it seemed he was able to do them all by himself. Yet, God still said that he needed a helper. Why is this?

As we have already established, it was not to meet his spiritual needs. He already had a spiritual relationship with God. He walked and talked with God on a daily basis. He had fellowship with God regularly. And, there was no sin between them.

So, God created Eve to meet the *physical* needs of the man. She was there to meet his physical desires, and help him as he lived for God.

She was to be a help to him, not a hinderance. Adam did not need a boss to tell him what to do. He needed someone that would willingly surrender her will to his, and be there for him, and help meet his physical needs. It was for this reason that God made marriage

In the Institution of Marriage, it was God who made the rules, and he also set up a system of authority. God's order for marriage in the Bible goes like this: The man is the *HEAD*, the woman is the *HELP*, and the children are the *HOPE*.

Let's look at these in order.

The Man is the Head

In Ephesians 5:23, in the context of marriage, we read, "**For the husband is the head of the wife, even as Christ is the head of the church...**"

Again Paul says this in 1 Corinthians 11:3, when he states:

> **But I would have you know, that the head of every man is Christ; and the head of the woman *is* the man; and the head of Christ *is* God.**

So, the order that God has set up is Christ first, then the man, and then the woman.

Of course, God the Father is the ultimate head according to the Bible. Read with me in 1 Chronicles 29:11:

> **Thine, O LORD, *is* the greatness, and the power, and the glory, and the victory, and the majesty: for all *that is* in the heaven and in the earth *is thine;* thine *is* the kingdom, O LORD, and thou art exalted as head above all.**

God the Father is the Head above all. And, it was God himself who instituted Marriage. So, we must listen to him, and what he says if we want to honor him. And, in the marriage relationship, the only way to do so, is for the man to be the head of the woman, just as Christ is the head of the Church.

So, in the marriage relationship, just as Christ is to be the head over the man, so too the man should be the head over the woman. And, the Bible says that she is supposed to be in subjection to him and under submission just as the man is to be to Christ.

In Genesis 3:16 we read these words:

Unto the woman he said, I will greatly multiply thy sorrow and thy conception; in sorrow thou shalt bring forth children; and thy desire *shall be* **to thy husband, and <u>he shall rule over thee.</u>**

Why would God set it up this way? Why did he allow the man to *rule over* the woman?

The answer is found in verse 13 of Genesis:

And the LORD God said unto the woman, What *is* this *that* thou hast done? And the woman said, The serpent beguiled me, and I did eat.

Eve was deceived by the Devil, and sinned by eating the forbidden fruit. Because of this, God's punishment on her was two fold: 1. *for her to have pain in childbearing,* and 2. *for her to be in subjection to her husband.* Her husband was to rule over her, so that he could protect her from sin and deception.

This is why God made the man as the Head. For, if a woman has no head, she is open for Satanic attack, and deception. She needs a head, someone to protect her from the wiles of the devil. God set up the man as the one to do just that, and man's responsibility as the *head* is to be a just leader, who keeps his wife safe, protected from evil.

Paul verifies the reason man was made the head in his epistle to Timothy. He writes:

1 Tim 2:14 And Adam was not deceived, but the woman being deceived was in the transgression.

1 Tim 2:15 Notwithstanding she shall be saved in childbearing, if they continue in faith and charity and holiness with sobriety.

It was the woman who was deceived, not the man. She *transgressed* or *sinned* because she was not with Adam. She was away from him, and that's when the Devil approached her and tricked her into doing wrong.

These verses also tell us that a woman will be saved in childbearing (kept from having so much pain) if she will willingly submit to the authority of her husband as her head.

It is true that there are some men that are an awful type of Christ, and they may not even be in subjection to Christ. But, the Bible still says that the woman is to be in subjection to her husband and to his position as the head of the family.

We have many corrupt judges in our land today. But, when we approach a judge in court, we are to address them as "Your honor." Why is this? Because we are showing reverence to the position. The judge himself might be a sorry rascal who lies, cheats, steals, and takes bribes. But, we still must honor his office. It is the same way in marriage with the headship of a man. The woman is to honor the position of head that the man is in, even if the man is not what he should be.

This, as we shall see, is important for a woman to remember, for it will help her in her role that God created her for, in order to be more of a help to her husband.

The Woman is the Help

As we've already seen, the woman was created to be a *helper* to her husband. But, most women today feel that they are degraded or that they are missing out on life if they subject themselves to the authority of a man. They think that they can do all a man can do, and ought to have the chance. They go to college, and get a job and career, and live their lives for themselves. And, in so doing, they go against the purpose of God for their lives, oftentimes missing out on the blessings of motherhood, and wifehood. A woman can only truly be happy as she helps the man. By knowing she is taking care of him, she sees that she is needed. And, by helping him, she is fulfilled by knowing that she is obeying the Lord.

By following God's word, and being in subjection to the man, the woman will not only be a blessing to her husband, but she will give honor to God as well. But, by rejecting God's ordained system of authority, she will live her life only to please herself. And if she marries, it will be for selfish reasons and the marriage will suffer because of it.

So, women, follow God's word and be fulfilled, or reject God's word and help yourself, but you'll be miserable in the long run; both in life, and at the day of judgment.

There are three good examples of godly women in the Bible, who desired to follow God's plan for their lives. They are Rebekah, Ruth, and Esther. Let's look briefly at all three of these.

When Eliezer came to *Rebekah*, the Bible says in Genesis 24:20 that she ran to get water for him and his camels. That is a good woman in the eyes of God, because she is a hardworker who wanted to *help* the man. She also wanted to get married and be a wife. And, when Eliezer asked her to go and marry Isaac, she answered in Genesis 24:58, "**I will go**."

No modern, liberated, selfish woman here. She was a good woman in the eyes of God because she wanted to fulfill the purpose in her life that God created her for.

Ruth is also a great woman in the word of God, and the only woman in the entire Bible that God calls *virtuous*. She too is a *hard worker*, and is *willing to do for others*. In Ruth 3:5, we read what Ruth said to her mother-in-law, "**…All that thou sayest unto me I will do**." This shows her meek and quiet spirit of submission.

Then as you read further down in Ruth chapter three, we find Ruth asks Boaz to redeem her, so that she can be his wife. (She asked him to marry her!) She also desired to be what a woman is supposed to be according to God's plan, and be a helper to the man.

And then we have to look at *Esther* as well. She is a wonderful woman, and was used by God to save Israel, her people, from destruction. But, she did not do it by her own power. She did it by her *obedience* to her husband, and her meek and quiet spirit. She is a great woman in contrast to Vashti in Esther chapter one, who was rebellious, and disobedient to the king's commands.

Clearly the Bible teaches that God created woman to be a help to the man. She was created for that very purpose, and the Bible gives us many examples of godly women and good wives.

However, far too many women today do not think this way. If married, they usually are not a help to their mate, as they only desire to do their own will, and fulfill their own personal agendas. These women are not following God's word, and are not what God created them to be. They need to read the Bible, and find some godly women, and try to live by their example. Otherwise, they'll end up deceived by Satan just like Eve was.

The modern Feminist Movement of our day has greatly destroyed the institution of marriage, as well as what it means to be a woman. They teach that a woman is her own person, and should not be under the "headship" of any. She should be in control of her own life, and live for herself. But, this goes against the very reason that woman was created.

Further, they downgrade men, and preach that they are animals after only one thing—S-E-X! This breeds hatred and contempt for the man, and because of this, women today look at men as someone they must compete with. Thus, it becomes a competition where the woman competes with the man to try to prove that she is as good as, if not better than, the man.

The modern liberated woman wants to know that she can do as much as, if not more, than a man can. She does not want his protection, rather to be free to do as she will. And, this mentality not only kills marriages, but keeps women from desiring to get married in the first place.

From the scriptures, we see that this modern Feminist Movement is only a lie of the Devil. In fact, he is the one who started this lie with Eve. For, the first thing that satan said was, "*Yea hath God said?*"

The Devil desired to cause doubt in Eve's mind to what God really said, and then undermine the way God set things up. He wanted Eve to be self-willed, independent, and freethinking. He wanted her to be free from her husband and his protection. But it wasn't because he cared about her. It was so *he himself* could get her under *his* rule and run her (better stated, *"ruin her"*).

But as we have seen, God set up marriage with the man as the head, and the woman as the help. This was God's design, so that the man could protect the woman from spiritual attack.

Satan is still active today in deceiving women into not being what they are supposed to be, for he knows by so doing, he can can destroy the family and the marriage relationship. And, this is exactly what he does in our day.

Notice what happened when Eve sinned. Satan came to her in the Garden of Eden and asked her what God said. Eve at first replied correctly that they should not *eat* of the tree in the midst of the garden, but then she added the words "**neither shall ye touch it.**" God never said that! He told Adam and Eve not to EAT of the tree. He never said don't TOUCH it. This shows that Eve must have thought about touching it, and this is why she added to God's word. She must have already been secretly thinking about rebelling against God, and flirting with something that God said was forbidden. She must have been wanting to go against God's commands. Satan saw this and tried to exploit it when he approached her in the garden.

As they spoke, Eve later subtracted from God's word when she removed the word "**freely**" from God's command. Eve, then, was the first "Bible corrector." She *added to* and *took away* from God's words!

This is exactly what the Modern Feminist Movement does today, as it seeks to "liberate" women from God's plan for their lives, while it seeks to undermine God's authority. It appeals to women who are flirting with going against God's word. And, it makes them desire to be their own "gods" (what Satan said that Eve would be if she would only go against God's command.

The Devil made Eve think that she was missing out on something wonderful that she deserved. He appealed to her that she needed *knowledge* (**the desire to make one wise**). And, *experience* (**good for food**), and he made her think that she would be *smarter* if she went against God (**ye shall be as gods**).

And, this is the same lie of the Devil today preached to women through the modern Feminist Movement, which teaches women that they need an education (knowledge), and a career (experience), and a salary (in order to make their own way and do as they please). And, to be married will only keep her from these things. So, why should a woman want to get married? According to the feminists, she has so many things she must do in her life, as she needs to "*go and better herself.*" She must get a job, and work hard to compete with the man, and then try to beat him.

But, according to the Bible, this way of thinking is a great hinderance to Biblical marriage. And, if a woman thinks this way and then get's married, she will not want to be under the "headship" of a man. She'll want to be the head herself. But in marriage you cannot have two heads. (Someone once said, "*Something with two heads is a MONSTER!*" How true!)

A woman who wants to run her own life and rule herself will not be God's woman, following God's set up in the marriage relationship. Rather than being a *help* to her husband, oftentimes, she'll be a *hinderance*. She also will be a corrupting influence upon her own children.

That brings us to our next topic.

The Children are the Hope

Finally, we must realize that the children are the *hope* of the marriage relationship, and must be taught how to have a good, sound marriage when they grow up.

The children are the only hope that we as Christians have. If we fail to raise our children for God, then they will go to the world for their doctrine and teaching on the subject of marriage. And, as we have seen, the world rejects God and his teaching. For this very reason society, morals, and marriages are being destroyed in our country, and yea in the world today.

The Bible is clear that the world wants our kids. The government has set up a system of public schools to indoctrinate our children with lies. They have kicked out the Bible, the ten commandments, and prayer from the schools. They have taught them that they are nothing but animals, and because of this, they end up living like such. Sadly, as the children go the way of the world, so goes God's institution of marriage out the window.

In Exodus 10:10 and 11, we find Pharaoh, king of Egypt (a type of the Devil), telling Moses to let the men of Israel go free, but don't take the children with him. Pharoah wanted them left with him, so he could train them in the ways of the Egyptians. And, this is exactly what the Devil wants us as Christians to do today. He wants us to leave our children in Egypt (a type of the world), so that the Devil can train them. But, let me say that if you send your children to an Egyptian school, they *will* come back with Philistine ways!

It has always been, and always will be the Devil's plan to intice, corrupt, and destroy our children. Thus, a Christian family has an awesome responsibility in raising their children for God. For their kids are the only hope that Christianity and the marriage relationship has.

Proverbs 22:6 says, "**Train up a child in the way he should go: and when he is old, he will not depart from it**." And, the word *train* means in order to teach someone something, you have to be doing it yourself.

God knows we need more Christian fathers and mothers who will honor God's institution of Marriage, and show their children what it is to live for God, and stay together. Divorce in the parents, will usually lead to divorce in the children. Kids learn by example. We need to live for God, and live our lives according to the word of God, and teach our kids that they should do the same. If the marriage goes bad, the children will go bad as well. And, if the children go bad, so will the nation.

Chapter 5

Marriage as A Type of Christ and the Church

The biggest problem with married couples today, is that they do not realize that marriage is a type of Christ and the church. As we have already seen, God instituted the marriage relationship for many reasons. But, for a Christian, it was to show them their relationship with Jesus Christ.

The Bible says that when a person accepts Christ as their Saviour, they are born again. And, they are a part of *the bride of Christ* (Rev. 21:2,9, and 17), which the scripture calls *the Church* (Colossians 1:18, 24). Paul said this to the Church in 2 Corinthians 11:2:

> **For I am jealous over you with godly jealousy: for I have espoused you to one husband, that I may present *you as* a chaste virgin to Christ.**

Christ is our espoused husband if we are Christians. He is our fiancée. And, we the Church (all born again believers) will marry him someday at the Marriage of the Lamb.

But, as far as God's concerned we are already his. We are already married in his eyes. We are one flesh (Col. 1:24). We as Christians are already a part of the body of Christ (1 Corinthians. 12:27)! And this is unchangeable.

To see and understand how this applies to Marriage, we must look at the definitive chapter on the subject. This is, of course, is Ephesians chapter 5, verses 22-33:

vs 22 Wives, submit yourselves unto your own husbands, as unto the Lord.

vs 23 For the husband is the head of the wife, even as Christ is the head of the church: and he is the saviour of the body.

vs 24 Therefore as the church is subject unto Christ, so *let* **the wives** *be* **to their own husbands in every thing.**

vs 25 Husbands, love your wives, even as Christ also loved the church, and gave himself for it;

vs 26 That he might sanctify and cleanse it with the washing of water by the word,

vs 27 That he might present it to himself a glorious church, not having spot, or wrinkle, or any such thing; but that it should be holy and without blemish.

vs 28 So ought men to love their wives as their own bodies. He that loveth his wife loveth himself.

vs 29 For no man ever yet hated his own flesh; but nourisheth and cherisheth it, even as the Lord the church:

vs 30 For we are members of his body, of his flesh, and of his bones.

vs 31 For this cause shall a man leave his father and mother, and shall be joined unto his wife, and they two shall be one flesh.

vs 32 This is a great mystery: but I speak concerning Christ and the church.

vs 33 Nevertheless let every one of you in particular so love his wife even as himself; and the wife *see* that she reverence *her* husband.

We can learn a whole lot about marriage from these verses. Right away, we see that God is a stickler for *obedience*. The first verse states that a woman is to *submit* to (or obey) her husband. Again it says this in vs 24 and adds, "**in every thing**." Remember that the man in the marriage relationship is a type of Christ, and the woman is a type of the Church, or Christians. And, God demands obedience from his bride—the Church.

God wants us to obey Him and His words in everything. There is a reason for this. God wants people to follow his rules in order to have a good marriage the way God ordained it. But, if we make up our own rules in marriage, and are not obedient to God, then our marriages will fall apart. We must follow God, and His way completely, and "**in every thing**," in order to be better Christians.

What is God's way? As we've already seen, in the Institution of Marriage, God set up a hierarchy, with *the man* in charge as the leader, *the woman* in submission to him, and *the children* under them both. In other words, as stated in the last chapter, the man is the *head* (vs 23), the woman is the *help* (Genesis 2:18), and the children are the *hope*. This is God's plan. It always has been, and always will be. And, God wants us to follow his rules not only because it's right, but also to fulfill the type of Christ and the church.

Let's look at Genesis 3:16 once more:

Unto the woman he said, I will greatly multiply thy sorrow and thy conception; in sorrow thou shalt bring forth children; and thy desire *shall be* **to thy husband, and he shall rule over thee.**

Here God says the man is supposed to be the *ruler* of the family. He's to be the king of his own castle. Why? Because Christ is the ruler of his Church! That is so simple.

Does Jesus Christ desire his Church to rule over him and tell him what to do? Does he allow his bride to control him? No. He is the Ruler and King, and he is in charge. What he says goes. And, as a good Christian, you are supposed to obey him.

Now, notice that God starts out these verses in Ephesians chapter five speaking to the woman. And, in every case in Paul's epistles, when he is speaking on the home, the first admonition is always to the woman. (See also Col. 3:18, and even 1 Peter 3:1). There is a reason for this. The Bible says in 1 Tim. 2:17, "**Adam was not deceived, but the woman being deceived was in the transgression**."

When God made human beings, he made man first, and then the woman. She was created secondly. She was a secondary creation. That does not downgrade her in anyway. But, it does show that she is not equal to the man. In fact, the Bible says that the woman is the "**weaker vessel**" in 1 Peter 3:7. It does not say that she is *weak*. It only says that in comparison to the man, the woman is a weaker vessel.

She is weaker for several reasons. First of all, she is weaker *physically*. Her body is different than a man's body. A man is made for working outdoors. But, a woman's body is not as strong as a man's. She's more delicate and petite than he is.

Secondly, a woman is weaker than a man *emotionally*. When God made man, he made him in His image. And, if you read your Bible, you'll see what God is. He's compassionate, but firm. He's loving, but also immovable in his stand for truth. With God, it's either right or wrong, up or down, right or left, black or white. God judges according to facts, and not according to feelings. He does not allow his emotions to sway his decisions. And, this is how God made man as well.

But, a woman is much different. She is usually led by her emotions. She decides what she wants by how she feels. Whatever mood she's in determines her reaction to something. She is emotional, and sometimes that makes her irrational. She needs a man to be over her, to take care of her, and calm her down in times of trouble, and discouragement. She needs his comfort in despair, as well as his kind, and uplifting words to make her feel wanted. She needs the man to make decisions for her based on what's right, and not on what feels good. Decisions must always be based only upon facts, not feelings!

Finally the woman is a weaker vessel because the Bible says in our verse above in 1 Timothy, that she is *easily deceived*. When the Devil came to tempt and steal and destroy in the garden, he came to Eve. Why? Because he saw that she was led by her emotions, and not by facts. And, if he could make her feel good, or present something to her that would please her, then he could cause her to fall into sin. And, this is exactly what Satan did.

We have a saying in America that goes like this: *"Men fall in love with what they see, and women fall in love with what they hear."* This is so true. A woman is swayed by what she hears. To be won, she is to be wooed with words. Some call it *"sweet talking"* a woman to get something from her. The Devil knew this and used flattery of great swelling words to deceive Eve.

For this very reason, God said that the woman is to be in obedience to the man. Because by herself, she can be easily deceived. She needs a protector, a head, to keep her from deception. Someone that loves her and wants to keep her from sin.

Now, before you get mad, let me say that everything I just said is not only true about the man and the woman relationship, but also about Christ and the Church! We need Christ as our head (Ephesians 5:23), to keep us from deception, sin, and hurt. We need his comforting words to heal us and help us in our valleys and our sicknesses. We are the weaker vessel, in comparison, and are in need of a protector, ruler, and provider. We are a needy people, we are easily deceived by our emotions, and need God to show us the truth from his word! We need to obey Him, and by so doing we will be kept free from the deception of the devil.

Hopefully by now you can see that in God's plan of marriage, women should obey their husbands like Christians should obey Christ. In so doing, she fulfills the type of Christ and the Church. But, if she doesn't obey her husband, she breaks the type of Christ and the Church, and dishonors God.

Now, let's look as some more verses in the Bible about this. In Titus 2:5, God commands women to be... **"discreet, chaste, keepers at home, good, obedient to their own husbands, that the word of God be not blasphemed."** Did you get that? That Bible says in the end of this verse that if a woman *disobeys* her husband, it's BLASHPEMY and she BLASPHEMES the word of God!

If this is true in marriage (a type of Christ and the Church) then that means that when we as Christians disobey God, we blaspheme his word as well! (God help us!)

So, if a woman (the weaker vessel) will get a hold of these Biblical truths, and realize it's for her own betterment to find and follow a husband, she will make a wonderful wife, and make God happy.

Nowadays, in this crazy mixed up world, most women don't like to be told what to do by a man, because they have been told by a wicked, devil controlled system they don't have to. They claim that a man, when he is given power over her, will try to control or take advantage of her. She screams, *"I don't want to be oppressed!"* But, the Bible says a woman is commanded by God to obey her husband. It all boils down to who she wants to obey. She'll either obey God, her husband, and the Bible, or she'll follow the Devil and his world system, obeying him above God. She just needs to decide who she will serve.

But, if she finds a good husband who is obedient to God, and loves her like Christ loved the Church and gave himself for it (vs 25), then the woman will never have to worry about a man trying to degrade her or mistreat her. She should choose a husband according to God's word, and choose wisely. Proverbs 14:1 says, "**Every wise woman buildeth her house: but the foolish plucketh it down with her hands**." And, women should get wisdom from God's word, and not from the world.

But the question arises so often today in so-called Bible Believing churches, "*What if the man asks her to do something wrong? Should she obey him?*"

The answer is found in the Scriptures. When God wrote in Ephesians 5:24, "**Therefore as the church is subject unto Christ, so** *let* **the wives** *be* **to their own husbands <u>in every thing</u>**," he meant it. If you don't believe it, you are not a Bible Believer. If you reject it, you are a Bible rejecter. If you disobey it, you are a Bible blasphemer. It's that simple.

When God set up the marriage relationship, he set the man up as the head of the home. He is the ruler of it. He is in charge. But, with this authority, comes responsibility as well. He is responsible to one person, and one person only — God. And, at the Judgment Seat of Christ, he will give an account of how he treated his wife, and what he asked her to do (Hebrews 13:17). He will give account to God if he asked his wife to sin.

The woman, however, is accountable to the man. And, she will give account to God for one thing, and one thing only. Whether or not she obeyed her husband. For by so doing, she is obeying God who told her to obey and submit to her husband. When she obeys him and his office, she is fulfilling the type of the Church obeying God. When she disobeys her husband, she is telling the Church that it is okay to disobey God, and it is okay to blaspheme his word.

Therefore, what an awesome responsibility a woman has! She is an example to her husband in how to obey God. She also is an example to her children in how to obey their father, and ultimately God the Father. And, she is also an example to the angels, showing them by her subjection that she is a godly woman (See 1 Corinthians. 11:9,10 for more on that). So, the woman has a tremendous job to do as a wife, and must realize that if she fails, then she is teaching disobedience to others.

We need more godly women today that will go against the world's teaching and doctrines, and will willingly obey God, and his word by obeying their husbands! And, the only thing that will make a woman want to obey her husband, is love.

In Ephesians 5, we see that love is essential. Six times the word "*love*" is used, and three times its a command for the man. Nowhere in the passage is the woman told to love her husband. She is only told to obey. Why? Because it's a lot easier to obey someone that loves you. And, if a man truly loves his wife, he wouldn't ask her to do anything that he wouldn't do himself.

God's love to us (the bride of Christ) was manifested on the cross of Calvary, and because of that marvelous love, he gave his life for us. Because of this, we should want to serve him the more in return.

In marriage it should be the same way. A man should love his wife enough to die for her. And she should want to live for him in return.

Now, let's look at some verses about this. In Genesis 3:6 we read these words:

And when the woman saw that the tree *was* good for food, and that it *was* pleasant to the eyes, and a tree to be desired to make *one* wise, she took of the fruit thereof, and did eat, and gave also unto her husband with her; <u>and he did eat</u>.

From the preceding chapters, we have already seen that Eve was the one who sinned first. She *added to* and *subtracted from* God's word. She was beguiled, and deceived into eating of the fruit, and disobeying God. And, in this verse we see that Eve gave the fruit to her husband, and he ate as well. But, why did he eat of the fruit? Was he deceived? No, the Bible clearly says that the man was not deceived, but the woman. So why did Adam eat of the fruit? The only conclusion that one can truthfully and scripturally come to is that Adam loved Eve enough to die for her, and with her.

And, this is what Jesus did for us. He loved us enough to die for us. The Bible proves this as it likens Jesus unto Adam in 1 Corinthians. 15:45. The Bible says it like this:

And so it is written, The first man Adam was made a living soul; the last Adam [Jesus Christ] *was made* a quickening spirit.

Adam is a type of Christ in the Bible. Both he and Christ die for their bride. They both face sin in a garden. They both are made in the image of God. They are both called the son of God. And, both of them have their side opened for their bride.

So, in order for us to begin to understand the love that Christ has for his bride—the Church, we must recognize that it is a type of the love that a man is supposed to have for his wife. Let's analyze this in more detail.

What is love according to the Bible? Well there's several good verses that show what love is. One is found in John 15:13. It says, "**Greater love hath no man than this, that a man lay down his life for his friends.**" This verse says that the greatest love is to be willing to die for someone. But, look with me at another verse if you will.

John 3:16 says, and I quote:

For God so loved the world, that he gave his only begotten Son, that whosoever believeth in him should not perish, but have everlasting life.

This verse shows us that love is *giving*. True love is not only willing to die for someone, but it is also willing to live for that person, and give them your life as well. It's easy to die for someone. That wouldn't take very long if it was done clean and fast. But, it's sure hard to live 40, 50, 60 years for one person and give them your life. This is what Paul calls "dying daily." And, what is love? It is giving yourself to someone else. And, this is what marriage is on both parts.

The problem with the world today is that they do not understand what love is. They confuse love with lust. Love says, *"What can I give to this person?"* Lust cries out, *"What can I get from this person?"* And, this is why so many marriages in America, and in our Churches, and yea even in the world are not working out. Because their foundation is lust, instead of love.

Build the foundation of your Marriage on love, and it shall never crumble. Build the foundation on lust, and it shall never grow. In fact, it will fail as lust increases, and seeks another. We must learn that Marriage is founded on love. And, love is not just a feeling or an *emotion*. Love is an *action*.

Let's look at some more verses in Ephesians chapter 5 to see this. In these passages, we see that *sacrifice* is necessary in love, and in Marriage. Verse 24 says again to the woman, "**Therefore as the church is subject unto Christ, so let the wives be to their own husbands in every thing.**" Do you realize that it takes some sacrifice to be in subjection to someone? It's hard to obey and allow someone to rule over you. But, God said to do it. It's the same with Christ and the Church. Paul said this to the church in Romans 6:19:

...for as ye have yielded your members servants to uncleanness and to iniquity unto iniquity; even so now yield your members servants to righteousness unto holiness.

It's not easy to go against that flesh. It's a sacrifice to do what God says at times, when your flesh wants to do the opposite. It's not easy to live for God and yield to him and his commands. But, God wants our obedience because it pleases him. And, a woman will never please her husband and have joy in herself as a wife and a Christian until she learns to sacrifice her will, to the submission of the man. For only by doing this will she please God and her husband.

It's also important for a man to sacrifice in marriage. Verse 25 says, "**Husbands, love your wives, even as Christ also loved the church, and gave himself for it.**" Christ gave himself for the church. He sacrificed Himself and His wants and desires for us. And, by so doing, He became the ultimate sacrifice on the cross for all sinners. But, it wasn't without a cost.

Jesus had to say this to God in Luke 22:42, "**Father, if thou be willing, remove this cup from me: nevertheless not my will, but thine, be done.**" And, that's what a sacrifice is. It's putting down your will, and doing something for someone else, even when you don't want too! A man needs to sacrifice some of his desires and wants, and do some things for his wife. And, a woman needs to sacrifice her wants for the commands of her husband if a marriage is to work!

But, nowadays we live in such a characterless society that no one wants to sacrifice anything. They are selfish. The motto of people today is, *"Me first, you next – Maybe!"* But, God's word says a marriage is to have sacrifice on both parts. The man is to sacrifice for his wife as Christ did for the Church, and the woman is to make herself "**a living sacrifice**" (Romans 12:1,2) just as we are to be for Christ, and submit herself to her husband.

The very best way, then, to explain marriage is by the following statement: The man is to _SACRIFICE_ for the wife, and the wife is to _SUBMIT_ to the husband.

This is what Christ did for us, and what we are supposed to do for him.

Another thing we see in these verses in Ephesians chapter 5 is that marriage is a joining of two into one. Verse 31, states, "**For this cause shall a man leave his father and mother, and shall be joined unto his wife,**

and they two shall be one flesh." You can't join something when you're still joined to something else. And, for a man to join his wife and vice versa, they have to sever themselves from their parents. In other words, they need to move out of their parent's house and away from their parent's authority.

Many marriages have been wrecked by a woman's parents who still try to tell their little darling what to do, against the wishes of her husband. And, many marriages have been destroyed by men who listen to advice from Mommie and Daddie instead of the Bible. Or men who won't leave father and mother, and end up driving away their mate who married *him*, and not his parents!

I'm not saying that the Bible doesn't say, "**Honor thy father and they mother...**" But, I am saying that you can honor them better from a distance rather than living with them. More often that not, it will cause problems.

So, God says that marriage is a joining of a man and a woman together. Amos 3:3 says, "**Can two walk together, except they be agreed?**" For a man and woman to join themselves together, they need to be in agreement.

And, the most important thing, is that they both be Christians. 2 Corinthians 6:14,15 commands:

> **Be ye not unequally yoked together with unbelievers: for what fellowship hath righteousness with unrighteousness? and what communion hath light with darkness?**
>
> **And what concord hath Christ with Belial? or what part hath he that believeth with an infidel?**

A saved man, and an unsaved woman, or vice versa will have many problems, because the unsaved mate will usually not understand or want to follow marriage as a type of Christ and the Church. They will usually only want what they can get out of marriage and not want to give and understand the sacrifice of Christ. They will marry for lust, or for emotions, rather than for love, and for the desire to give all they can to the other person.

This brings me to my next and final point about marriage. And, this question must be addressed: *"Why is marriage so cheapened in America today, especially in churches?"* The answer is that churches are not separated from the world. And, because of this, many worldly ideas and secular beliefs about marriage are creeping into our churches.

Someone once said, *"The church is getting worldly, and the world is getting churchy."* That's about right. Everyone wants enough religion to appease their conscience, and then they go on living their life anyway they want. And, because the Church is so worldly today, most "Christians" (I use the term loosely) don't take marriage seriously. Why is this? The answer is two fold. 1. Because the world doesn't take it seriously, and 2. Because Churches are not teaching what the Bible says about Marriage.

Instead of teaching God's word, Pastors in our land are teaching what a Psychiatrist, or a Psychologist, or a Counsellor thinks, instead of the Bible. They teach as doctrine, the traditions of man. And, they've made the final authority a man or an institution, instead of God and his holy word.

The lost world does not understand marriage. Because of this, unsaved people don't care much about it. Most of them in this world today just spend their time going from one "one night stand" to another. Their mentality is, *"Why get married to have sex when you can have it without marriage and with anyone you want?"* They are warped in their reality, and have been deceived just as the Devil deceived Eve.

Then to add to that problem, the Church has quit teaching what the Bible says about the Biblical Institution of Marriage. And, parents have quit using the Bible as their textbook. They have let the world train their children on the subject.

Schools today teach children that fornication is not wrong. It's only *"adult consent."* They teach the damnable doctrine of: *"If it feels good do it!"* And, *"what ever makes you happy, is okay!"* And, as a result, the doctrine of Marriage is debased, degraded, and frowned upon.

We live in a society today of people that are going against the Bible and God's word! When God said, **"Thou shalt not commit adultery."** He meant it! But, as society continues in its downward spiral of immorality, the institution of marriage will fade away more and more.

Jesus said this in Luke 17:26,27 about the last days:

And as it was in the days of Noe, so shall it be also in the days of the Son of man.

They did eat, they drank, they married wives, they were given in marriage, until the day that Noe entered into the ark, and the flood came, and destroyed them all.

It's not about following God's plan of one woman and one man together for life, it was a party where men and women came together and stayed together until they found someone else that could please their wicked sexual desires. They would then divorce and marry someone else (i.e. get a piece of paper), but it was only because it was the traditional thing to do. It wasn't for love. It wasn't to honor God. It was to please the flesh. Then they would do it again and again. It was only to please and gratify the desires of their flesh. It was not an honorable institution to keep moral fidelity in the populace.

This is why God destroyed the earth in Noah's day. There was too much emphasis on the sexual aspect of marriage, and not enough on the spiritual picture of God and man. In other words, marriage was a sex party rather than a moral obligation to your mate which honored God. And it's sad but true, today's society of loose morals and easy divorcism has crept into our Churches. There are more divorces in Churches today than any other time in America. Why? Because pastors are not preaching about marriage from the Bible and explaining what it is! And, if they do attempt to preach about it, they usually exalt the woman above the man (i.e. magnify the Church above Christ). Truly we are in the Laodicean church age.

We need to get back to sound morals in this country. We need to recognized marriage as a type of Christ and the Church, and we need to preach the necessity of staying together. Christ told the Church, **"I'll never leave thee nor forsake thee!"** This mentality ought to be preached and taught in the aspect of Marriage as well!

In Summary

God said that men and women were to marry one another in order to keep them from fornication. They were to come together as one flesh with God honored in their vows. They were to fulfill the type of Christ and the Church, and in so doing understand their relationship with Christ. They were commanded to stay together and love one another as a testimony to the world, and to their children that marriage is indeed honorable in all.

But, why is this not what's happening today? Why are there so many divorces, especially in so many Churches in our land? Why don't Christians obey God when they claim to love and follow him? I believe the answer is three fold. 1. People don't realize that Marriage is a covenant between man and God. 2. People don't look at marriage as a type of Christ and the Church, and 3. Christians don't live separated lives from the world.

If we could just show them what the Bible says about marriage, maybe they would see the truth, and the importance of staying together and working on making their marriages better. The old saying is: *"Marriage is what you make it."* And, how true this is. So, many today don't make any sacrifice, and far too many women won't submit to their husbands. Thus, the marriage ends up in divorce, and the spouses don't even care. But, God does!

And, God's desire is for them to remember the vow they made to their spouse, and keep it! No matter what! The Marriage vow says, *"In sickness or in health, as long as they both shall live!"* This is what Marriage was instituted to be.

Some erroneously say, "Marriage is 50-50," claiming it's 50% of the man's responsibility and 50%

the woman's responsibility to make the marriage work. But this is a twisted view of marriage. The truth is marriage is 100-100. That is, the husband should give 100% to his wife, just as the woman should give 100% to her husband, each one working together fulfilling their roles and responsibilities in the marriage relationship.

This brings us to our next chapter, "Duties Required in marriage," which gives us an overview of what each one should do for his mate.

Chapter 6

The Duties required in Marriage

Duties of the Man

Now, let's look at some of the duties of the husband in the marriage relationship, and see what God expects from him.

The first duty of the man is to *love* the woman. As we've seen in the prior chapter, love is more than just an emotion. Love is an action. It is giving. And, the man is supposed to sacrifice himself for his wife, and give her some things.

1 Peter 3:7 says this:

> **Likewise, ye husbands, dwell with *them* according to knowledge, giving honour unto the wife, as unto the weaker vessel, and as being heirs together of the grace of life; that your prayers be not hindered.**

This verse instructs the man to give honour unto his wife. Why? Because she is the weaker vessel. And, he should treat her as such. He should be good to her, and take care of her, and be a type of Christ to her. And, the verse goes on and says that if he does not, then his prayers will be hindered. Herein is an interesting thing. This verse says that God is looking out for the woman. And, if a man mistreats his wife, then God will not answer that man's prayers!

It is the duty of the man to treat that woman like Christ treats his Church. And, also he is commanded in this verse to dwell with her according to knowledge. In other words, he should know the Bible, and what it says about marriage in order to be sure he is fulfilling his type as a type of Christ.

If he is reading God's word, he'll learn how to love his wife. And, it's hard to mistreat someone that you love and care about. Because of this, God tells a man to love his wife many times in his word. Here are a few of those verses:

Ephesians 5:25 Husbands, love your wives, even as Christ also loved the church, and gave himself for it...

Ephesians 5:28 So ought men to love their wives as their own bodies. He that loveth his wife loveth himself.

Ephesians 5:33 Nevertheless let every one of you in particular so love his wife even as himself; and the wife *see* that she reverence *her* husband.

Colossians 3:19 Husbands, love *your* wives, and be not bitter against them.

God wants him to love her, because if he does, he's more willing to give, and sacrifice more for her. And, love is something that has to be given, even if it is not returned.

God loved us enough to die for us, even though he knew that there would be some that would reject him, and what he did for them at Calvary. But, he went to the cross anyway. His love was not determined upon whether or not we loved him first.

In the marriage relationship, it is the same way. A man must love his wife regardless of whether or not she is being what she should be. If the man only loves the woman when she is pleasing him, then when she disappoints him, he'll, as Col. 3:19 above says, "**be bitter**" against her. And, bitterness, and anger will seriously hamper the marriage relationship, not to mention his prayers to God.

The Bible says also in 1 Corinthians 7:3, "**Let the husband render unto the wife due benevolence: and likewise the wife unto the husband.**"

That word *benevolence* means *kindness, charity, goodness done with the desire to promote the happiness of another*. And, if the man has these attributes toward his wife, and vice versa, then they will keep from getting bitter at one another.

1 Corinthians 7:36 says that a man should "**behave himself**" toward his wife. He should be a Gentleman. And treat her with lovingkindness.

And finally, we read this in Ephesians. 5:29, "**For no man ever yet hated his own flesh; but <u>nourisheth</u> and <u>cherisheth</u> it, even as the Lord the church**."

God says that the husband should nourish and cherish his wife. The word *nourish* means *to promote growth*.

The husband should help his wife to grow in the grace and knowledge of Jesus Christ. He should have devotions with her, and pray with her, so that she will grow stronger as a Christian.

And, the word *cherish* means *to treat with tenderness and affection, to ease or comfort, to hold as dear*. The man should strive to do just that. And, if he really cherishes his wife, he would never look at another woman. He would never jeopardize his marriage relationship and go commit adultery with someone else. He would love his wife, and want to come home to her alone.

Now, let me briefly list some things that the Bible says a man is supposed to be, and give a verse for it, and then we'll move on to the duties of the woman.

What the Man is to be:

1. A Protector of his wife

1 Pet 3:7 **Likewise, ye husbands, dwell with *them* according to knowledge, giving honour unto the wife, as unto the weaker vessel, and as being heirs together of the grace of life; that your prayers be not hindered.**

2. Lover of his wife

Ephesians 5:25 **Husbands, love your wives, even as Christ also loved the church, and gave himself for it;**

3. Head of his wife

1 Corinthians 11:3 But I would have you know, that the head of every man is Christ; and the head of the woman *is* the man; and the head of Christ *is* God.

4. Teacher

1 Corinthians 14:35 And if they will learn any thing, let them ask their husbands at home: for it is a shame for women to speak in the church.

5. Saviour

Ephesians 5:23 For the husband is the head of the wife, even as Christ is the head of the church: and he is the saviour of the body.

Duties of the Woman

Some of the duties of the woman in the Marriage relationship have been covered in the earlier chapters. God wanted her to be a help to the man, and by so doing she must be in subjection to the man and obedient. But, let's look at these verses as well:

Ephesians 5:22 Wives, submit yourselves unto your own husbands, as unto the Lord.

Colossians 3:18 Wives, submit yourselves unto your own husbands, as it is fit in the Lord.

Titus 2:5 To be discreet, chaste, keepers at home, good, obedient to their own husbands, that the word of God be not blasphemed.

1 Pet 3:5 For after this manner in the old time the holy women also, who trusted in God, adorned themselves, being in subjection unto their own husbands:

1 Pet 3:6 Even as Sara obeyed Abraham, calling him lord: whose daughters ye are, as long as ye do well, and are not afraid with any amazement.

Unmistakably, from these verses, and many others that we have covered, it is God's will for a woman to obey her husband. This is God's design in marriage, and the very reason that he made woman. It was for her to *help* him.

Now, look at Col. 3:18 above, and read the last seven words. Many a Pastor has taken these words and twisted them, and wrested them to their own destruction, and that of their Marriage. They take the words, "**as it is fit in the Lord**," and say that that means a woman only has to obey her husband if it is "**in the Lord**." This is called "selective obedience," and in truth is not obedience at all.

They further state that if a husband asks his wife to do something unscriptural, then she doesn't have to obey him. Because, they say, it is not "**fit in the Lord**."

There are several things wrong with this philosophy and marriage destroying doctrine.

The first way we know that this is a heretical teaching is by looking at the cross reference in Ephesians. 5:22.

It starts out saying the exact same thing, then it ends by saying, "**as unto the Lord**." In other words women, You are to obey your husband as you are to obey God. And, by obeying your husband, you are obeying the Lord, because in Ephesians 5:24, God said, "**Therefore as the church is subject unto Christ, so *let* the wives *be* to their own husbands in every thing**." When God said for the woman to obey the man in everything, he meant it.

So, if we look again at Colossians 3:18 in light of the scriptures, we see that it says, "**Wives, submit yourselves unto your own husbands, as** [or *because*] **it is fit in the Lord.**"

Why submit to your husband ladies? Because it is fit in the Lord to do so! This is what God told you to do in his word.

Another reason why it is unscriptural to teach a woman that she can disobey her husband in certain areas, is that it breaks the type of Christ and the Church. God too wants us to obey him "in everything" as it says in Ephesians 5:24. To teach the opposite is to blaspheme God's word, and to shun his institution of marriage.

Lest you think I am being chauvinistic, and a hater of women, let me tell you there is a great book about this subject written by, of all people, a woman. The book is called, "Me Obey Him?" And, in the book she shows that when God says to obey your husband, that's exactly what you should do!

It's God's way, or the highway. You can do it his way, and the marriage will work. Or you can do it your way, and the marriage will be destroyed, God's word will be blasphemed, and your children will follow in your footsteps.

So, from all of this we see that one of the main duties that God expects of a woman in the marriage is to be obedient to her husband, for by so doing she obeys God.

Now, let's look at some other duties of the woman. 1 Peter 3:1- 4 say this:

1 Pet 3:1 Likewise, ye wives, be in subjection to your own husbands; that, if any obey not the word, they also may without the word be won by the conversation of the wives;

1 Pet 3:2 While they behold your chaste conversation coupled with fear.

1 Pet 3:3 Whose adorning let it not be that outward adorning of plaiting the hair, and of wearing of gold, or of putting on of apparel;

1 Pet 3:4 But let it be the hidden man of the heart, in that which is not corruptible, even the ornament of a meek and quiet spirit, which is in the sight of God of great price.

There is a lot in these verses, and many duties found for a woman in the marriage relationship. The first thing we see is that a woman's conduct (obedience) to her husband will do more to help him do right than if she preached to him.

Many a woman feels that God has called her to be a preacher. But, God says that is not so to be. She is to win her husband by her obedience. The man isn't going to listen to her words if she tries to teach or preach to him. It is not in his nature. He looks at her conduct and way of life. If she is walking the Christian life, and doing what God says, that will do more to convict him, than if she preached a seven point Homiletical outline. And, as we have already seen about the man, it is his duty to know God's words already, and follow it.

Further, the woman can make a man love her even more by whether or not she is in subjection to him. And, in verse 2 we see that when a husband sees that his wife fears God enough to obey him, (by obeying her husband), then that will really get to a man. A man will be less likely to ask a woman to sin when he sees that she is a spiritual woman. And, what makes her spiritual is not her preaching, but is her "**meek and quiet spirit**" which pleases God (vs 4).

Another passage that shows us what a woman should do to please God is in 1 Timothy chapter five. We read:

1 Tim 5:14 I will therefore that the younger women marry, bear children, guide the house, <u>give none occasion to the adversary to speak reproachfully</u>.

1 Tim 5:15 For <u>some are already turned aside after Satan</u>.

These verses tell us why a woman should have a quiet and meek spirit about her. The reason is that if she is loud and boisterous, then Satan will be able to get a hold on her, and deceive her (Read Proverbs 7 for further details about a harlot), and then he'll cause her to sin. The louder she is, the less listening she'll do to her husband. But, if she is quiet, and meek, and willing to obey, then she will be what God wants her to be in the Marriage

Relationship. And, if she's not, then she will usually end up leaving her husband. And, God commands against that in 1 Corinthians 7:10. I quote:

And unto the married I command, *yet* **not I, but the Lord, Let not the wife depart from** *her* **husband:**

So, the duties of the woman are tremendous. She is to be obedient. She is to have a quiet and meek spirit. She is to be a help to her husband, and not preach to him, but show him by her obedience to him how he should be in his relationship to God. She is to stay with him, and never depart from him. She is to be a blessing to him all the days of his life.

Oh how few women there are like this in America today. As we have seen, women have been taught by the government, the schools, and the women's lib movement, that this is not their place. They teach that women should strive to be someone, and make something of their lives. The world shouts, *"Go to college, have a career, live for yourself! Exalt your gender! But, down the 'repressive' men who want to take advantage of you and control you!"*

This is the lie of the Devil that is being preached to woman everywhere today. And, just as Satan beguiled Eve, so now is he deceiving womanhood. And, these most pernicious fables are destroying our nation, our homes, and our Churches.

One needs to realize that the nation will never rise above the families that are in that nation. And, a Church will never be any greater than the homes that are represented in that assembly. So, goes the home, so goes the nation. So goes the family, so goes the Church.

And, if the Church is not preaching and teaching the Institution of Marriage as God set it up, then man will not know the glorious type that marriage is of Christ and the Church.

This is why Paul penned these words nearly 2000 years ago, and they should ring forth like a bell in churches throughout our land today:

2 Corinthians 11:3 But I fear, lest by any means, as the serpent beguiled Eve through his subtlety, so your minds should be corrupted from the simplicity that is in Christ.

Marriage is so simple if we just follow God's plan. But, to do that, we must realize that we are in a mess, and we need to kick the Devil, and his anti-biblical, satanic doctrines about marriage out of our Churches, and go only by what God says, and be faithful to his word.

Now let's look at what the woman is supposed to be in the marriage relationship according to the scriptures.

What the Woman is to be:

1. <u>Helper</u>

Genesis 2:18 **And the LORD God said, *It is* not good that the man should be alone; I will make him <u>an help</u> meet for him.**

2. Crown

Proverbs 12:4 **A virtuous woman is a crown to her husband: but she that maketh ashamed is as rottenness in his bones.**

3. Glory

1 Corinthians 11:7 **For a man indeed ought not to cover his head, forasmuch as he is the image and glory of God: but the woman is the glory of the man.**

4. Precious

Proverbs 31:10 **Who can find a virtuous woman? for her price is far above rubies.**

5. A Good Thing

Proverbs 18:22 **Whoso findeth a wife findeth a good thing, and obtaineth favour of the LORD.**

Let me further say, to those of you that are married, you must work together in your marriage relationship, and do your duties to your spouse and to God in order for the marriage to work. No one ever said it'd be easy. Marriage is a lot of work! But, the more you put into it, the more you get out of it. You both must be what God told you to be and do your duties as a good husband or wife.

And, that brings us to our next topic...

Equal Duties of both Man and Woman

Now in our study of the duties in the Marriage relationship, we come to the equal duties of both the man and the woman. These are to be done by both sides, as well as the duties that God gave to each one individually.

First we see that God says this in

1 Corinthians 7:4 The wife hath not power of her own body, but the husband: and likewise also the husband hath not power of his own body, but the wife.

1 Corinthians 7:5 Defraud ye not one the other, except it be with consent for a time, that ye may give yourselves to fasting and prayer; and come together again, that Satan tempt you not for your incontinency.

This is talking about the sexual aspect of Marriage. And, the Bible is a very practical book if you'll read it and obey it. It says that in the sexual part of marriage, a man's body is not his own. It belongs to his wife. And, the woman's body is not her own, it is the man's. They are not to *defraud* one another's sexual needs.

There are several reasons why God said this. First, to show us once again the type of Christ and the Church. 1 Corinthians 6:19, and 20 say this to us the church,

"What? know ye not that your body is the temple of the Holy Ghost *which is* in you, which ye have of God, and ye are not your own?

For ye are bought with a price: therefore glorify God in your body, and in your spirit, which are God's."

God says to those of us that are saved, that we are not our own. We are bought with a price. We are Christ's. And, Christ is ours. We are in Him, and He is in us. What a picture of salvation! And, we have a wonderful Saviour in Jesus Christ our Lord!

The other reason that Paul would write to tell married couples not to defraud each other is to keep adultery from happening. If a man and a woman would realize that they each have some needs that must be meet, and it were their desire to do so, then their marriage relationship would be fantastic. Their needs would always be met, and they would have no desire to find someone else. They would stay with their mate.

Too many marriages today end in divorce because one partner is not fulfilled sexually, and does not have his or her needs met. So, what do they do? They seek other avenues to please the desires of the flesh. Usually, they will find someone else who will please them. But, by so doing they have broken their vow, they have sinned against their own flesh, and they have displeased God.

Another duty required by both man and woman is found in 1 Peter chapter 3. Actually there are many duties listed that will help a couple have a good Marriage. They are as follows:

1 Pet 3:8 Finally, *be ye* all of one mind, having compassion one of another, love as brethren, *be* pitiful, *be* courteous:

1 Pet 3:9 Not rendering evil for evil, or railing for railing: but contrariwise blessing; knowing that ye are thereunto called, that ye should inherit a blessing.

If married couples will keep these commandments, and do their duties, they will do well. And, they will inherit a blessing.

Marriage doesn't have to be a curse. It can be spectacular, wonderful, and fulfilling. It can be fun, satisfying, rewarding, and exciting all at once. But, in order for it to be these things, each partner must be willing to take part in their duties, and be faithful in so doing. Otherwise, undoubtedly the marriage will be on the rocks, and quite possibly end in the grievous sin of divorce.

Chapter 7

Divorce

Now that we've finished our study on Marriage, let's go to the Bible and see what it has to say about divorce. But, before we do, let's look at what the dictionary says about it.

The Webster's 1828 Dictionary defines divorce in the following way:

Divorce, *noun,*
1. *A legal dissolution of the bonds of matrimony, or the separation of husband and wife by a judicial sentence.*
2. *The separation of a married woman from the bed and board of her husband.*
3. *Separation; disunion of things closely united.*
4. *The sentence or writing by which marriage is dissolved.*
5. *The cause of any penal separation.*

Divorce, verb
1. *To dissolve the marriage contract, and thus to separate husband and wife.*
2. *To separate, as a married woman from the bed and board of her husband.*
3. *To separate or disunite things closely connected; to force asunder.*
4. *To take away; to put away.*

From these definitions, we see that the word "*divorce*" can be used for several things. It can be used in talking about a legal thing where a piece of paper is given which the government and the court system call "Divorce papers," but which God, in the Bible, calls "**a writing of Divorcement**."

Or, it can be used in talking about a dissolution or a dividing or cutting of one thing from another.

Let's look at the paper part of divorce first. The Bible uses the term "**Writing of Divorcement**" twice in the New Testament. It is in Matt. 5:31, and 19:7. In the context, Jesus is talking about something that was done in the Old Testament. It was something that was written in the law in Deuteronomy 24:1-4. It is called a "**bill of divorcement**" (see also Jeremiah 3:8), and it was allowed by the law. But, look at what Jesus says about it in Matt. 19:8,

> **Moses because of the hardness of your hearts suffered you to put away your wives: but from the beginning it was not so.**

God says that it was Moses who wrote divorce into the law, and in God's plan, it was not to be. God never put divorce into the marriage equation. As far as God is concerned, divorce should never take place! Look again at what God says in Mark 10:9,

What therefore God hath joined together, let not man put asunder.

The Bible is very clear that God hates divorce. He is against it, and never intended it to be, even from the beginning when he instituted marriage. God's plan never included one spouse divorcing the other with a writing or bill of divorcement. He also didn't want the spouse to divorce or put away, divide or unjoin themselves from the spouse by any other means either.

Let's look a little bit more about divorce and what it is. Most people think that it is just getting a piece of paper and once that's done, a person is divorced. But, just like marriage, there is more too it than just a piece of paper.

Reasons for Divorce vs. Causes of Divorce

Many preachers in America today teach that there are *reasons for* a person to actually get a divorce. Some say that if the man is a drunkard, or abusive, then the wife should divorce him. Others say if the woman is a tramp, or a whore than the man should start divorce proceedings against her. Then there are those that say you can get divorced whenever you want. They use the term "Irreconcilable Differences," and say, "*Well, too bad it just didn't work out.*"

Then there are those that say scripturally, there are only three reasons for Divorce. They are: 1. *Death*, 2.

Desertion, and 3. *Fornication*. Now, let's look at what the Bible says about these things.

1. <u>Death</u>.

According to our definitions of Divorce, some of the meanings of the word are *to separate*, *to disunite*, *to force asunder*. This is exactly what death does in a marriage when one spouse dies. Death *separates,* and <u>*disunites*</u> two married people. The one flesh of two joined together, is now only one again. And, the living partner is now at liberty to remarry to anyone, and at anytime he chooses. We can clearly see this in 1 Corinthians 7:39, which states:

The wife is bound by the law as long as her husband liveth; but if her husband be dead, she is at liberty to be married to whom she will; <u>only in the Lord</u>.

But, death is what caused the divorce itself. There were no divorce papers involved. It was the *cause* of the divorce.

2. <u>Desertion</u>.

Now we have a problem. It is not found anywhere in the Bible that a person can get divorced because a person separates from them. In fact, the contrary is true. We read this in 1 Corinthians:

1 Corinthians 7:10 And unto the married I command, yet not I, but the Lord, Let not the wife depart from her husband:

1 Corinthians 7:11 But and if she depart, let her remain unmarried, or be reconciled to *her* husband: and let not the husband put away *his* wife.

Here we are told by Paul, and by God who inspired him to write this, that a woman is not to depart (or separate) from her husband. And, a man is not to put away or separate himself from his wife. This is just not meant to be. If one spouse does leave, they are supposed to come back to their partner, and be reconciled, according to the Bible. God's plan holds no room for someone to willingly get a divorce from their mate.

3. <u>Fornication</u>.

Here we find something interesting. Jesus told us this in Matthew 5:32,

But I say unto you, That whosoever shall put away his wife, saving for the cause of fornication, causeth her to commit adultery: and whosoever shall marry her that is divorced committeth adultery.

People use this verse and say that it is an excuse for someone to get a divorce. They say that if one spouse adulterates with someone else, then the other has grounds to get *a writing of divorcement* against the adulterer, and marry someone else. Is this Biblical? Is this a loop hole in marriage? Should we try to get a spouse we don't like to go and cheat on us with someone else so we can then divorce them?

The answer is no. We most certainly should not! People take this teaching of "Reasons for divorce" and twist it. They say it means a person has a reason and a right to get a divorce from their spouse. And, I've seen far too many "Bible Believers" (so called) use this terminology to tell others that it is okay to get a divorce from their mate. They use the Bible to justify their sin of getting a *bill of divorcement* from their spouse.

Now, if you say that these are *"Reasons FOR,"* and teach that if a person separates or fornicates then you can biblically divorce them, you are wresting the scriptures to your own destruction! God said, and I'll quote it again, **"What therefore God hath joined together, <u>let not man put asunder</u>."**

God does not want men or women to divorce one another, especially Christians! God gives no *reasons for* a man to get a divorce from his spouse. He wants marriages to last, and stay together.

So, what do we do with these verses? The only thing we can do. Believe them! And, if you say they are *reasons FOR* a divorce, then you are teaching a person should get a divorce in certain cases. This is not what God wants. Jesus said, **"From the beginning it was not so!"**

But, you can say these are the *"Causes OF divorce."* If you remember the definitions of divorce, you'll remember that it is *a putting asunder*, *a separating,* or *a disuniting.* This will work in all three cases.

When a person dies, they are divorced (cut asunder, disunited) from their spouse at the moment of death.

When a person separates from his or her spouse, he is *disuniting*, or *putting asunder* his or her body from the other person for how ever long a period of time it may be (but they should be reconciled and come together again). When a person adulterates, he or she joins his or her flesh to someone else, and *unjoins* their body from their mate. These are what *cause* the divorce. But, these are not an excuse for a person to go and get a writing of divorcement.

Let's look at the following verses:

Mark 10:11 And he saith unto them, Whosoever shall put away his wife, and marry another, committeth adultery against her.

Mark 10:12 And if a woman shall put away her husband, and be married to another, she committeth adultery.

God says that a person that commits adultery, and joins their body with someone else, divorces that person. But when they remarry (i.e. make another vow) God does not honor it, because it dishonors his plan. And, God calls it adultery!

God's plan has and always will be, for one man, and one woman to come together and marry each other by binding themselves together under God, and to stay together, and never leave each other willingly, and only be separated by death. Death you can't help, but Separation and Fornication (i.e. Adultery) you can! And, God hates these.

The Bible has all the answers. In 1 Corinthians. 7:5 God says to the married:

Defraud ye not one the other, except *it be* with consent for a time, that ye may give yourselves to fasting and prayer; and come together again, that Satan tempt you not for your incontinency.

Isn't that practical? If a man and woman will realize that their body is not their own, and that they are each others, and if they will give themselves one to the other, then there would be no want for the other spouse to leave (separate), or to fornicate (or adulterate). Their needs would be met.

So, the Bible is clear that there are *Causes of divorce*, but not *Reasons for a divorce*. And, many justify their sin by saying, "*Well, I have a scriptural reason to divorce* (i.e. get divorce papers against) *my spouse*." But, God gives none whatsoever. God does not want anyone to divorce his or her spouse. But, if one spouse adulterates or dies, then a divorce has taken place.

How do you like that? Every one is going to be divorced someday if the Lord tarries. How? They are going to die. And, death is a divorce. But, this cannot be helped. But, fornication and adultery can! And, they ought not so to be.

Separation should not take place either! It divides asunder that "one flesh" of marriage for the time the partners are away from each other, and if they are not reconciled, then more often than not, one of the two spouses will join their flesh to someone else. And, in all actuality, this (not just the separation) is what causes the divorce. God despises this act of fornication and adultery because it breaks that vow of marriage that the husband and wife made one to another. God has always, and will always hate divorce, and he will never condone it.

But, immediately someone will stand up and say, "*But God divorced Israel in the Bible!*" And, when they say this, they are referring to Jeremiah 3:8. In this passage, it says that God gave Israel a "**bill of divorcement**." But, God did not divorce Israel, otherwise he would be a sinner, and, guilty of the very thing he told us not to do. He would be breaking the type of Christ and the Church himself. So, how do we reconcile this? We must read and believe the Bible.

Let's look at what God says in Isaiah 50:1:

Thus saith the LORD, Where *is* the bill of your mother's divorcement, whom I have put away? or which of my creditors *is it* to whom I have sold you? Behold, for your iniquities have ye sold yourselves, and for your transgressions is your mother put away.

At first glance, one would say, that God put her away, and that proves that God divorced Israel. And, then they may say, "*if God can get a divorce, then I can too!*"

But, look at the last part of the verse. It says that it was for her *transgressions* (adultery) that she is put away. It is very clear that it was Israel that put God away first. She divorced herself from him by her adultery and treachery (Jer. 3:20). Can you see that? Can you get that? Do you not understand? God is not for adultery. He hates it. In fact in Malachi 2:16, we read this. " **For the LORD, the God of Israel, saith that he hateth putting away.**" God hates it when a man or a woman divorces or puts away his wife. It's an abomination unto him, and goes against the very reason that God set up Marriage to begin with.

Let's look at some verses in Ezekiel chapter 16 that shed more light on this.

Ezekiel 16:15 But thou didst trust in thine own beauty, and playedst the harlot because of thy renown, and pouredst out thy fornications on every one that passed by; his it was.

Ezekiel 16:16 And of thy garments thou didst take, and deckedst thy high places with divers colours, and playedst the harlot thereupon: the like things shall not come, neither shall it be so.

Ezekiel 16:17 Thou hast also taken thy fair jewels of my gold and of my silver, which I had given thee, and madest to thyself images of men, and didst commit whoredom with them.

According to these verses, we see that it was Israel that divorced God first by her idolatry (which the Bible calls spiritual adultery). She played the harlot, she committed whoredom. She joined herself to Baal. She is the one who divorced herself from God. And, God then gave her a "bill" of divorcement to show her what she had already done. It was not a piece of paper from God so that he could get a divorce from her. The divorce happened when Israel joined herself to pagan idols. God just gave her the *writing of divorcement* to show her what she had already done to Him.

And, it doesn't end there. Look at the book of Hosea. God tells the prophet Hosea to go and marry a whore, so that he could know what it feels like to have someone commit adultery on him like Israel did to God. So Hosea did as God commanded. And, sure enough, she returned to her whoredom, and adultery. Then in verse 2 of Chapter 2 the Bible says that Hosea is no longer married to her because of her adulteries. But, he still wishes her to quit her sin.

In the passage, we find that it's a type of God and Israel, as well as Hosea and his wife Gomer.

Let's read this verse:

Hosea 2:2 Plead with your mother, plead: for she *is* not my wife, neither *am* I her husband: let her therefore put away her whoredoms out of her sight, and her adulteries from between her breasts;

This is God speaking to Israel as well as Hosea speaking to Gomer. And, the Bible says that he is not her husband. Why? Because she divorced him by her whoredoms. She joined herself unto another. This is what caused the divorce. But, her flesh joining flesh to others does not constitute a marriage to them. It will never be honorable in the eyes of God, because it is adultery.

As far as God is concerned, she still (because of her vow) belongs with Hosea, just as Israel belongs with God (Isa. 54:5). Look at these following verses in Hosea,

Hosea 2:17 For I will take away the names of Baalim out of her mouth, and they shall no more be remembered by their name.

Hosea 2:18 And in that day will I make a covenant for them with the beasts of the field, and with the fowls of heaven, and *with* the creeping things of the ground: and I will break the bow and the sword and the battle out of the earth, and will make them to lie down safely.

Hosea 2:19 And I will betroth thee unto me for ever; yea, I will betroth thee unto me in righteousness, and in judgment, and in lovingkindness, and in mercies.

Hosea 2:20 I will even betroth thee unto me in faithfulness: and thou shalt know the LORD.

Hosea 2:21 And it shall come to pass in that day, I will hear, saith the LORD, I will hear the heavens, and they shall hear the earth;

Hosea 2:22 And the earth shall hear the corn, and the wine, and the oil; and they shall hear Jezreel.

Hosea 2:23 And I will sow her unto me in the earth; and I will have mercy upon her that had not obtained mercy; and I will say to *them which were* not my people, Thou *art* my people; and they shall say, *Thou art* my God.

This passage of scripture has all sorts of things in it. But, the gist of the message is that God is willing to take back Israel and he says he is going to do so. He will betroth her unto him again (vs. 20). And, look at vs 18, where God says he'll make a new covenant with her (a vow). This is Him marrying her again.

Israel as a nation in the picture divorced herself from God, but God loved her so much, that he was willing to take her back. He was going to uphold his vow, and yea even make another, even if she wasn't.

In the passage, we see that Hosea didn't fair so well. Gomer divorced him, and wouldn't ever come back. So, God told him to marry again in chapter 3, and he does so. This is scriptural remarriage. And, we'll get to that in the next chapter. But, we must realize from these verses, and all the verses in the Bible what divorce is. It's when someone's flesh is put asunder. And, that can happen two ways: By death, or by adultery. And, we have established that God is against divorce, and it displeases him when it happens.

The sad fact is that it does happen. And, even though it's never God's will, it will continue to happen. Many people have, do, and will continue to divorce one another.

In the 1950's and even before, the word "divorce" used to be a bad word in America among moral, law-abiding citizens. But, in the day in which we live, the opposite is true. The sad truth is that in America today, divorces are rampant not only in our country, but in our Churches as well.

In 1977 the U.S. census bureau gave the following figures about Divorce.

In 1920, 1 divorce for every 7 marriages
In 1940, 1 divorce for every 6 marriages.
In 1960, 1 divorce for every 4 marriages.
In 1972, 1 divorce for every 3 marriages.
In 1977, 1 out of 2 marriages end in divorce.

And, those statistics are well over twenty years out of date. In the year 2000, the divorce rate went up to over 80%.

What has happened in the last fifty years to make something at one time so unthinkable, now quite acceptable? Why are 8 out of 10 Marriages ending in divorce in America?

As aforementioned, the first reason is that we have quit listening to good, sound Biblical preaching on the subject. Instead of going to the Bible, we have "counsellors" and "Christian psychologists" who claim to be experts on the subject of marriage. But, do they have the answers? Can they help stop the number of rising divorces in America? How about Television? All you see on the subject today are "Divorce Courts" which show and even condone divorces. How does this help the problem?

The answer is that the only help to this problem is found in the Old King James Bible that this country was founded on. It tells us what marriage is, what it's for, and how to make it work! It also has some things to say about divorce.

As we have seen, Marriage is a covenant between two people before God that they will stay together til "death do them part." However, in America today we are far from that vow. In 1999, 7 out of 10 marriages in America ended in divorce. That shows that we have a nation full of liars. America is full of covenant-breakers. People who will make a vow, and break it, and not even feel bad about it.

We are seeing the fulfillment of Paul's prophecy in the following verses:

2 Tim 3:1 This know also, that in the last days perilous times shall come.

2 Tim 3:2 For men shall be lovers of their own selves, covetous, boasters, proud, blasphemers, disobedient to parents, unthankful, unholy,

2 Tim 3:3 Without natural affection, trucebreakers, false accusers, incontinent, fierce, despisers of those that are good,

2 Tim 3:4 Traitors, heady, highminded, lovers of pleasures more than lovers of God;

2 Tim 3:5 Having a form of godliness, but denying the power thereof: from such turn away.

2 Tim 3:6 For of this sort are they which creep into houses, and lead captive silly women laden with sins, led away with divers lusts,

2 Tim 3:7 Ever learning, and never able to come to the knowledge of the truth.

This is the reason that divorce has become so wide spread, and so acceptable.

The mentality of most people in America is, "*If it doesn't work out, there's always divorce.*" But, this was not God's plan. God's plan was for a man and a woman to marry and stay together til death. Once again, let's look at Matt. 19 and verse 8, which states: "...**Moses**

because of the hardness of your hearts suffered you to put away your wives: but from the beginning it was not so."

God says here that in the Old Testament, a man could divorce his wife. But, he that did so, did it because his *heart was hardened* to what was right. Look with me at what Moses penned in Deuteronomy 24:1:

> **When a man hath taken a wife, and married her, and it come to pass that she find no favour in his eyes, because he hath found some uncleanness in her: then let him write her a bill of divorcement, and give *it* in her hand, and send her out of his house.**

How cold, how heartless! How little love, and respect for God's word does a man (or a woman) have that would divorce his mate. And, God says that the reason divorce is so rampant in the world today is because of the hardened heart of man. Man's heart is deceitful, and desperately wicked (Jeremiah 17:11). And, the harder and colder it gets, the more divorces we'll see.

God's plan from the beginning was for one man and one woman to get together and stay together. Again let's look at what Jesus said Matt 19:4-6:

> **And he answered and said unto them, Have ye not read, that he which made *them* at the beginning made them male and female,**
>
> **And said, For this cause shall a man leave father and mother, and shall cleave to his wife: and they twain shall be one flesh?**

Wherefore they are no more twain, but one flesh. What therefore God hath joined together, let not man put asunder.

Divorce was not God's plan from the beginning. And, it's not God's plan or desire now. So, as you read this book, and read the Bible, remember what God said about the subject, and do what he says in order to honor him, and be different from the world. You should try to be an example to others and show that marriage can work. It will work. It must work. But, it will only work if it's done according to God's plan.

Let's look at several more verses, and we'll close our study of divorce. And, then we'll see what the Bible says about remarriage.

Let's look first of all at Absalom, David, and the ten concubines. In 2 Samuel 16, we read these verses:

2 Sam 16:21 And Ahithophel said unto Absalom, Go in unto thy father's concubines, which he hath left to keep the house; and all Israel shall hear that thou art abhorred of thy father: then shall the hands of all that are with thee be strong.

2 Sam 16:22 So they spread Absalom a tent upon the top of the house; and Absalom went in unto his father's concubines in the sight of all Israel.

The Bible tells us Absalom went in unto his father's concubines and committed adultery with them. And, by so doing, he showed all Israel that there was no connection between himself, and his father. How is that? By separating (divorcing) them from their husband (David). And, that act of adultery unjoined David's body from his concubines, and divorced them from him.

Then in 2 Samuel chapter 20 when David returns to Israel, we read these words:

2 Sam 20:3 And David came to his house at Jerusalem; and the king took the ten women *his* concubines, whom he had left to keep the house, and put them in ward, and fed them, but went not in unto them. So they were shut up unto the day of their death, living in widowhood.

Some would say that they were widows indeed, as because they were joined to Absalom sexually, they were then *his* wives. And, when he died, they were widowed. But, the Bible does not say this. They were not married to Absalom. The act of flesh on flesh did not join them in marriage, but in adultery. It made them divorced from David. And, when David returned to Jerusalem, he did not want to touch them since they had been with his own son.

So, they lived out their days as though they were in "widowhood" although they were not widows. Their true husband David (whom they more than likely had a vow with) was not dead. But, he never came nigh unto them again. Why? Because they had been divorced from him.

Finally, let's close this chapter with John chapter 4, Jesus is talking to the Samaritan woman at the well. And, in verses 16-18 we read these words:

Jesus saith unto her, Go, call thy husband, and come hither.

The woman answered and said, I have no husband. Jesus said unto her, Thou hast well said, I have no husband:

For thou hast had five husbands; and he whom thou now hast is not thy husband: in that saidst thou truly.

Here Jesus asks the woman if she is married. She replies, "No." And, according to the rest of the verse, we find that she is currently living with a man in adultery. But, God says she has had five husbands before that. It does not say she *has* five husbands. Jesus says to her, "**Thou hast had five husbands**" (past tense). Now how can this be? Well, according to our study on divorce, either all five of these husbands died, or they committed adultery against her. Or a mixture of both. We can not know for sure. But, according to the passage, the man she is with now is not her husband.

So, there was clearly several divorces in her life. But, we must realize that what ever happened in this poor lady's life, God's desire was for her to be married honorably, and not living in adultery. Plus, he didn't want her to be divorced.

Maybe her last five husbands committed adultery on her and went and joined themselves to someone else. Then according to the Bible, (as we shall see in the next chapter) she would be divorced from them, and able to be remarried. But, according to the vow, her first living husband and herself should have stayed together. And, should still be together for their vow's sake. This would be what God wants.

I use this illustration to say this. What a mess it is, and what a mess society becomes when a man and a woman are not faithful one to another. What a mess we have in the world, and even in our Churches today, when we do not follow God's plan for marriage. We need to preach to couples about faithfulness before they get married, and stress their importance of staying together. Otherwise you will have an even bigger mess in society.

Our country is full of busted homes, and broken marriages. It's filled with people who have hardened hearts toward God and his ordained system of marriage. We need so badly to get back to God's word. And, use it as our foundation, and build a home upon it.

Chapter 8

Remarriage

So far, we have studied what the Bible has to say about Marriage and Divorce, and now we will study what the Bible says about Remarriage.

According to God's words, there are only three scriptural reasons for someone to get remarried. The first is when death has occurred, and separated one spouse from another physically. The Bible clearly teaches that if a spouse dies, then the one left alive is at perfect liberty to remarry.

Romans chapter seven has this to say about it:

Romans 7:2 For the woman which hath an husband is bound by the law to her husband so long as he liveth; but if the husband be dead, she is loosed from the law of her husband.

Romans 7:3 So then if, while her husband liveth, she be married to another man, she shall be called an adulteress: but if her husband be dead, she is free from that law; so that

she is no adulteress, though she be married to another man.

It is not sin for a woman or a man to remarry another if their spouse dies. But, the Bible does put this stipulation on it – it must only be to another Christian.

Let's read 1 Corinthians 7:39 to see this. Paul tells us this:

1 Corinthians 7:39 The wife is bound by the law as long as her husband liveth; but if her husband be dead, she is at liberty to be married to whom she will; only in the Lord.

Then Paul adds this in 1 Corinthians 7:40, "**But she is happier if she so abide, after my judgment: and I think also that I have the Spirit of God.**"

He says that if a woman's husband dies, she would probably be happier if she didn't remarry. Why is this? Because as the weaker vessel, and more emotionally distraught, the woman would always compare her second husband to the first, and would have some problems in the marriage relationship. Plus, she would constantly be reminded that her first love was gone, and it would take some time for those wounds to heal.

The second reason for scriptural remarriage would be if the spouse was an unsaved person, and ran off and left his or her spouse. The Bible shows us this in 1 Corinthians chapter seven:

1 Corinthians 7:12 But to the rest speak I, not the Lord: If any brother hath a wife that

believeth not, and she be pleased to dwell with him, let him not put her away.

1 Corinthians 7:13 And the woman which hath an husband that believeth not, and if he be pleased to dwell with her, let her not leave him.

1 Corinthians 7:14 For the unbelieving husband is sanctified by the wife, and the unbelieving wife is sanctified by the husband: else were your children unclean; but now are they holy.

1 Corinthians 7:15 <u>But if the unbelieving depart, let him depart. A brother or a sister is not under bondage in such *cases*</u>: but God hath called us to peace.

Notice the Bible says that if an unsaved man or wife leaves their mate, then according to God, they are no longer in bondage to their vow. Why? because the lost person did not honor God in his vow, and as far as God is concerned he doesn't know better. But, please don't misunderstand me. That is not what should happen. If anything, they should stay together if the lost person is willing to. That is always the best scenario.

Notice also that it does not say that if a saved person departs, then the other Christian spouse is not under bondage. God does not want two saved people to leave one another because if anything, they should want to play their parts in the role of Christ and the Church, and be a testimony to the lost world.

So, what is a saved person to do if their saved spouse leaves them? The answer to this scenario is found in 1 Corinthians in the following verses:

vs 10 And unto the married I command, yet not I, but the Lord, Let not the wife depart from her husband:

vs 11 But and if she depart, let her remain unmarried, or be reconciled to her husband: and let not the husband put away his wife.

God says that a saved person should not depart from their spouse. But, if they do, then they are not to remarry, and they are to be reconciled to their spouse. This is God's word on the matter.

But, too often, not only does a Christian man or woman leave their partner, but they do it to commit adultery. And, as we have already seen, this causes the divorce.

This brings us to our final scriptural reason for someone to remarry, that is in the case of adultery.

Jesus said this in Matthew 5:32,

But I say unto you, That whosoever shall put away his wife, saving for the cause of fornication, causeth her to commit adultery: and whosoever shall marry her that is divorced committeth adultery.

God says it's not right to put away your wife if you are a man. But, if she has fornicated with another man, and committed adultery, against her husband, then the man is at liberty to remarry. This is what Jesus says. Why? Because that spouse has divorced him or herself from the other one, and according to Jesus and the Bible, the other spouse is able to marry again if they so desire.

But, it's always better if they get back together for their vow's sake, and to honor God. And, also in the case of children, it is better for their parents to forgive and forget if at all possible, so that those kids will have their real parents to raise them.

Oh, what a mess it becomes when one spouse is unfaithful to the other! What bitterness, hatred, and anger it causes! And, it usually will destroy the home, and the children. God give us more people that will stay together in faithfulness in the marriage relationship for Jesus' sake!

We need more women who'll obey God's word, and do their best to fulfill their role as a type of the bride of Christ. God give us women who will try to be a help to their husbands, and serve them like we are to serve God.

God give us more saved, spirit-filled men that will make up their minds to rule their roost, and be a type of Christ to their wives, and children. May they say with Joshua, **"But as for me and my house, we will serve the LORD."**

For the only way to strengthen our Churches, and our nation is to build strong families, and this can only happen by following the precepts that God has set forth in his holy word.

So, this ends our study on Marriage, Divorce, and Remarriage. I hope it was a blessing to the reader, and a help to them in their Marriage relationship. My prayer is that the man will do his best to be a type of Christ, and the woman will love and obey the man like God told us to love and obey him.

I'd like to leave you with the words to an old hymn entitled, "A Christian Home." This should be every Christian's goal and prayer for their home.

> O give us homes built firm upon the Saviour,
> Where Christ is Head and Counsellor and Guide;
> Where every child is taught His love and favor
> And, give his heart to Christ the crucified:
> How sweet to know that thou his foot-steps waver
> His faithful Lord is walking by his side!
>
> O give us homes with godly fathers, mothers,
> Who always place their hope and trust in Him;
> Whose tender patience turmoil never bothers,
> Whose calm and courage trouble cannot dim;
> A home where each finds joy in serving others,
> And, love still shines, tho days be dark and grim.
>
> O give us homes where Christ is Lord and Master,
> The Bible read, the precious hymns still sung;
> Where pray'r comes first in peace or in disaster,
> And, praise is natural speech to every tongue;
> Where mountains move before a faith that's vaster,
> And Christ sufficient is for old and young.
>
> O Lord, our God, our homes are Thine forever!
> We trust to Thee their problems, toil, and care;
> Their bonds of love no enemy can sever
> If thou art always Lord and Master there;
> Be Thou the center of our least endeavor
> Be Thou our Guest, our hearts and homes to share.

Summary of What the Bible says about Marriage

The Origin of Marriage:

Genesis 2:18 And the LORD God said, *It is* **not good that the man should be alone; I will make him an help meet for him**.

Ecclesiastes 4:9 Two *are* **better than one; because they have a good reward for their labour.**

Ecclesiastes 4:10 For if they fall, the one will lift up his fellow: but woe to him *that is* **alone when he falleth; for** *he hath* **not another to help him up.**

Ecclesiastes 4:11 Again, if two lie together, then they have heat: but how can one be warm *alone?*

Ecclesiastes 4:12 And if one prevail against him, two shall withstand him; and a threefold cord is not quickly broken.

What Marriage is:

Hebrews 13:4 <u>Marriage is honourable in all</u>, and the bed undefiled: but whoremongers and adulterers God will judge.

Mark 10:6 But from the beginning of the creation God made them male and female.

Mark 10:7 For this cause shall a man leave his father and mother, and cleave to his wife;

Mark 10:8 <u>And they twain shall be one flesh</u>: so then they are no more twain, but <u>one flesh</u>.

Mat 19:6 Wherefore they are no more twain, but one flesh. What therefore God hath joined together, let not man put asunder.

Ephesians 5:31 For this cause shall a man leave his father and mother, and shall be joined unto his wife, and they two shall be one flesh.

What Marriage is for:

1 Corinthians 7:2 Nevertheless, <u>to avoid fornication</u>, let every man have his own wife, and let every woman have her own husband.

1 Corinthians 11:9 Neither was the man created for the woman; but <u>the woman for the man</u>.

Genesis 2:20 And Adam gave names to all cattle, and to the fowl of the air, and to every beast of the field; but for Adam there was not found <u>an help meet</u> for him.

Hosea 2:19 And I will betroth thee unto me <u>for ever</u>; yea, I will betroth thee unto me in <u>righteous</u>ness, and in judgment, and in <u>loving</u>-kindness, and in mercies.

Hosea 2:20 I will even betroth thee unto me in <u>faithfulness</u>: and thou shalt know the LORD.

Ephesians 5:25 Husbands, love your wives, even <u>as Christ</u> also <u>loved</u> the church, <u>and gave</u> himself for it;

The Order of Marriage:

Ephesians 5:23 For <u>the husband is the head of the wife</u>, even as <u>Christ is the head of the church</u>: and he is the saviour of the body.

1 Corinthians 11:3 But I would have you know, that the head of every man is Christ; and <u>the head of the woman is the man</u>; and the head of Christ is God.

1 Corinthians 11:12 For as <u>the woman is of the man</u>, even so is the man also by the woman; but all things of God.

Genesis 3:16 Unto the woman he said, I will greatly multiply thy sorrow and thy conception; in sorrow thou shalt bring forth children; and thy desire shall be to <u>thy husband</u>, and he <u>shall rule over thee</u>.

1 Pet 3:1 Likewise, <u>ye wives, be in subjection to your own husbands</u>; that, if any obey not the word, they also may without the word be won by the conversation of the wives;

1 Pet 3:5 For after this manner in the old time the holy women also, who trusted in God, adorned themselves, <u>being in subjection unto their own husbands</u>:

Ephesians 5:24 Therefore as the church is subject unto Christ, <u>so let the wives be to their own husbands in every thing</u>.

1 Corinthians 14:34 Let your women keep silence in the churches: for it is not permitted unto them to speak; but <u>they are commanded to be under obedience, as also saith the law</u>.

Ephesians 5:22 <u>Wives, submit yourselves unto your own husbands</u>, as unto the Lord.

Colossians 3:18 <u>Wives, submit yourselves unto your own husbands</u>, as it is fit in the Lord.

Duties of the man:

Ephesians 5:25 Husbands, <u>love your wives</u>, even as Christ also loved the church, and gave himself for it;

1 Pet 3:7 Likewise, ye husbands, <u>dwell</u> with them <u>according to knowledge</u>, <u>giving honour unto the wife</u>, as unto the weaker vessel, and as being heirs together of the grace of life; that your prayers be not hindered.

Ephesians 5:28 So ought men to <u>love their wives</u> as their own bodies. He that loveth his wife loveth himself.

Ephesians 5:33 Nevertheless let every one of you in particular so <u>love his wife</u> even as himself; and the wife see that she reverence her husband.

Colossians 3:19 Husbands, <u>love your wives</u>, and be not bitter against them.

1 Corinthians 7:3 Let the husband <u>render unto the wife due benevolence</u>: and likewise also the wife unto the husband.

Ephesians 5:29 For no man ever yet hated his own flesh; but <u>nourisheth and cherisheth</u> it, even as the Lord the church:

1 Corinthians 7:36 But if any man think that <u>he behaveth himself</u> uncomely toward his virgin, if she pass the flower of her age, and need so require, let him do what he will, he sinneth not: let them marry.

Duties of the woman:

1 Pet 3:6 Even as <u>Sara obeyed</u> Abraham, calling him lord: whose daughters ye are, as long as ye do well, and are not afraid with any amazement.

Titus 2:5 To <u>be discreet, chaste, keepers at home, good, obedient to their own husbands</u>, that the word of God be not blasphemed.

1 Corinthians 7:4 The wife <u>hath not power of her own body</u>, but the husband: and likewise also the husband hath not power of his own body, but the wife.

1 Corinthians 7:5 <u>Defraud ye not one the other</u>, except it be with consent for a time, that ye may give yourselves to fasting and prayer; and come together again, that Satan tempt you not for your incontinency.

1 Corinthians 7:10 And unto the married I command, yet not I, but the Lord, <u>Let not the wife depart from her husband</u>:

1 Corinthians 11:10 For this cause ought the woman <u>to have power on her head</u> because of the angels.

1 Corinthians 11:15 But if a woman <u>have long hair</u>, it is a glory to her: for her hair is given her for a covering.

1 Pet 3:3 Whose adorning let it not be that outward adorning of plaiting the hair, and of wearing of gold, or of putting on of apparel;

1 Pet 3:4 But let it be the hidden man of the heart, in that which is not corruptible, even the ornament of a <u>meek and quiet spirit</u>, which is in the sight of God of great price.

1 Tim 5:14 I will therefore that <u>the younger women marry, bear children, guide the house, give none occasion to the adversary to speak reproachfully</u>.

1 Tim 5:15 For some are already turned aside after Satan.

Equal duties:

1 Pet 3:8 Finally, be ye all of one mind<u>, having compassion one of another</u>, love as brethren, be pitiful, <u>be courteous</u>:

1 Pet 3:9 <u>Not rendering evil for evil, or railing for railing</u>: but contrariwise blessing; knowing that ye are thereunto called, that ye should inherit a blessing.

What the man is:

1. <u>Protector of his wife</u>

   1 Pet 3:7 Likewise, ye husbands, dwell with them according to knowledge, giving honour unto the wife, as unto the weaker vessel, and as being heirs together of the grace of life; that your prayers be not hindered.

2. <u>Lover of his wife</u>

   Ephesians 5:25 Husbands, love your wives, even as Christ also loved the church, and gave himself for it;

3. <u>Head of his wife</u>

   1 Corinthians 11:3 But I would have you know, that the head of every man is Christ; and the head of the woman is the man; and the head of Christ is God.

4. Teacher

1 Corinthians 14:35 And if they will learn any thing, let them ask their husbands at home: for it is a shame for women to speak in the church.

5. Saviour

Ephesians 5:23 For the husband is the head of the wife, even as Christ is the head of the church: and he is the saviour of the body.

What the Woman is:

1. Help

Genesis 2:18 And the LORD God said, It is not good that the man should be alone; I will make him an help meet for him.

2. Crown

Proverbs 12:4 A virtuous woman is a crown to her husband: but she that maketh ashamed is as rottenness in his bones.

3. Glory

1 Corinthians 11:7 For a man indeed ought not to cover his head, forasmuch as he is the image and glory of God: but the woman is the glory of the man.

4. Precious

Proverbs 31:10 Who can find a virtuous woman? for her price is far above rubies.

5. Weaker Vessel

1 Pet 3:7 Likewise, ye husbands, dwell with them according to knowledge, giving honour unto the wife, as unto the weaker vessel, and as being heirs together of the grace of life; that your prayers be not hindered.

6. A Good Thing

Proverbs 18:22 Whoso findeth a wife findeth a good thing, and obtaineth favour of the LORD.

A Good Marriage Proposal:

Psalm 34:3 O magnify the LORD with me, and let us exalt his name together.

A Good Marriage Vow for the woman:

Gen. 24:58 And they called Rebekah, and said unto her, Wilt thou go with this man? And she said, <u>I will go</u>.

A Good Marriage Vow for the man:

Hebrews 13:5 ...<u>I will never leave thee</u>, nor forsake thee.

Epilogue

After writing this book, many have read it and asked me, *"But what if I'm already divorced? What do I do now?"* My only answer to them is to put it all under the precious blood of Jesus Christ and start right now by living for the Lord and doing right. If there is no hope of reconciliation with their mate that they are divorced from, then they should make sure that they learn more about what God says about marriage and do everything in their power to make sure that if they do remarry, their new marriage will not end in divorce as well.

Many have tragically told me, *"My wife or husband divorced me and there was nothing I could do about it."* This is an awful thing, but is something that takes place quite frequently nowadays because of the loose divorce laws in our land. The only thing I can tell those to whom this has happened is to do all they can to reconcile with that person. If that person will not return after you've tried every effort to get them back, then leave it in God's hands. If you do decide to remarry, then make sure it is scripturally (to someone in the Lord), and that you do everything in your power to make sure you fulfill the type of Christ and the Church in that new relationship.

The author of this booklet recognizes that there exists in many churches today the mentality of "looking down" upon divorced people. And he wishes to address this problem by saying *"These things ought not so to be!"* Yes it is true that we live in a day and age of apostasy where many preachers not only encourage divorces, but have even been divorced themselves. These things ought not so to be either! I believe we should preach against divorce for any and every reason with all the fervor and power that we can muster!

But I also believe that it is our responsibity to pray for and help our Christian brothers and sisters in Christ whose spouses have defrauded them, and in their cold, wicked, selfish hearts have divorced them. I say we should love them and comfort those who have been defrauded. We should do all in our power to be there for them in their time of distress, and instruct them from the scriptures what they should do to make sure this terrible tradgedy will never take place again. We are commanded the following in Galatians 6:1 and 2:

1 Brethren, if a man be overtaken in a fault, ye which are spiritual, restore such an one in the spirit of meekness; considering thyself, lest thou also be tempted. 2 Bear ye one another's burdens, and so fulfil the law of Christ.

We should not look down upon those whose mates have left them as "second class Christians" as some churches do. We should feel sorry for them, and before we cast a stone, think that according to the wicked laws of our country our spouse could do the same to us if they ever so desired without us being able to do anything about it.

We should do even more to encourage them that if they can't reconcile with their mate for their vow's sake, then to find the right mate that they can marry and stay with the rest of their lives. Divorce should never be an option! Sadly, many have taken place. Thus, it is the job of the Preacher, Pastor, and Church to help those that have been divorced to understand more properly what the Bible says about the subject so that another divorce will never take place in that person's life. Not only is a Christian who gets a divorce a bad testimony to the lost and dying world, but they are also a bad testimony to their children and the Church. We should do all we can to see that a divorce never takes place in the first place! And, if they have already taken place, we should do everything in our power to reconcile the two parties to come back together for their vow's sake. If this is out of the question (which usually is the case in this wicked age of apostasy and carnality in which we live). Then we should stress that the divorced live for God. And if they remarry, then we should preach that they do so only in the Lord and with someone who will agree to do their responsibilites in the marriage according to the word of God.

If someone in our church is the *divorcer* and not the *divorcee*, then we must preach that they repent of their wicked and vile sin of divorcing their mate and encourage them to turn to God to try to make up for their sin. If they cannot reconcile with those they divorced, then they must put their sin under the blood of Jesus Christ and then determine in their hearts never to make the same mistake again.

Truly we live in a twisted, ungodly, and evil day and age. Because of this, we are in a mess. Divorces are rampant and divorce rates are continuing to grow each day.

We need to get back to the Bible and its teaching about marriage in order to have any hope whatsoever of seeing this change.

There are several things that you dear reader must do in order to honor God and His insitution we call Marriage.

First, you must follow God's words and do what He says in order to have a sucessful marriage.

Second, you must teach your children what the Bible says about the subject and make sure that when they marry, it is only *in the Lord* and with the attitude that it is forever! Divorce as an option should never enter into their minds!

Third, you must teach those who have suffered a divorce, that it's not the end of the world. There is hope at the end of the rainbow. And, if they seek to be remarried, you must help them to make sure that they enter into this vow with complete understanding of what marriage is, and what God expects of them according to the Bible. The only way to do this is for them to see the necessity they have to fulfill their role as a type of Christ and the Church.

Finally, if you know someone who with a cold and bitter heart divorced their spouse, you should reprove and rebuke them with all longsuffereing and doctrine, and show them that they have broken God's type of Christ and the Church.

A WORD OF ENDORSEMENT ABOUT THIS BOOK, "WHAT THE BIBLE SAYS ABOUT MARRIAGE, DIVORCE, AND REMARRIAGE,"
by Robert Breaker III:

I met brother Breaker as he was on deputation in 2001. As he and I discussed marriage, he has shown me to be a great example of a man looking to have a Biblical Marriage. This is his book.

I highly recomment this material as I will be using it here at my church in marriage discussions and 'counseling' for the Book. Great material!

It should help a young man and young woman start their marriage with the Book and it should help 'rescue' a marriage that has not gone by the Book, and it should also rekindle the fire of any marriage that has strayed from the Book!

Naturally, this study will also be good for those who stubbornly refuse to choose to have a marriage designed God's way – at least they will know what they are rebelling against when they choose to go to the counseling of the world.

- Mike Paulson
Former Pastor of Bible Believers Baptist Church
Touchet, WA

ABOUT THE AUTHOR

Robert Ray Breaker III is a King James Bible Believing Independent Baptist. His father led him to the Lord on July 29, 1992 in Milton, Florida.

A few years later he enrolled in the Pensacola Bible Institute and graduated there in 1998 with a Bachelors of Divinity.

While attending Bible School, Robert pastored, Garcon Point Baptist Church for a short time.

Two weeks after graduation, Robert went to Honduras, where he eventually became a Missionary for seven years on the field, planting several churches.

Today Robert is a member of an Independent Baptist church in Monterrey, Mexico, and travels extensively throughout Central, South, and even North America fulfilling his God-called ministry as a Missionary Evangelist to the Spanish-speaking people.

He also desires to reach his own English Speaking people in this day and age of apostasy, compelling them to return to the old time way, and stand firmly on the Biblical doctrines of salvation, sanctification, and the holy scriptures.

Bro. Breaker also runs BREAKER PUBLICATIONS, a small printing ministry, focusing on printing good, sound, doctrinal works founded on the Scriptures, not on tradition.

Other Works by the Same author:

The "Heresy" of the Sinner's Prayer

Hey, Where's the Blood?

The Importance of the Blood of Jesus Christ

Biblical Study Notes on Various Topics for Bible Believers

Why I am more than Just a Fundamentalist!

Why I am a Baptist

A Brief History of the Spanish Bible

The History and Truth about the Spanish Bible Controversy

The Spanish Bible and Those Courageous Men Behind its Inception

The History and Truth about the Modern Gomez Spanish Bible

These books and more are availabe at my website:
www.rrb3.com

Brought to you by:

Breaker's

Publications

740 Mike Gibson Lane
Milton, Florida 32583

Email: Robertbreaker3@hotmail.com
Website: www.rrb3.com